Packing by the Book

R.J. Corkum Nyks

Published by:

Bookit Publishing Ink
PO Box 382
Madison, Va 22727

Designed by: Kevin Osborn, Research & Design,Ltd., Arlington, Virginia

Produced by: Charles O. Hyman, Visual Communication, Inc.,
                Washington, D.C.

Edited by: Rebecca Barns, Charlottesville, Virginia
                Elizabeth Krijgsman, The Netherlands

Cover
photograph: Eric Long, Gaithersburg, Maryland

Printed and
bound by: Koninklijke Wöhrmann BV Zutphen, The Netherlands

ISBN: 0-9657337-0-X

First edition: R.J. Corkum Nyks © 1997
Text and photograph copyright © 1997 Corkum Nyks

To order more copies:

Contents

What to Pack – Section I

PART
1

WHAT TO PACK FOR "TOURS"
WITH TRAVEL TIME OF 7 DAYS OR LONGER

WHAT TO PACK FOR "GREAT ESCAPES"
WITH TRAVEL TIME OF 7 DAYS OR LONGER

WHAT TO PACK FOR SPORTS VACATIONS
WITH TRAVEL TIME OF 7 DAYS OR LONGER

What to Pack for "Dream Weekends"
WITH TRAVEL TIME OF A 3-DAY WEEKEND

PART 5 — WHAT TO PACK FOR TRAVEL WITH CHILDREN AND BABIES

PART 6 — WHAT TO PACK FOR TRAVEL WITH ADDITIONAL FAMILY MEMBERS: PETS

PART 7 — WHAT TO PACK FOR RENTAL VACATIONS

How to Pack – Section II

Ready to Go

Getting There

Before Leaving

Addresses

Publications and Books

Index

Packing by the Book

Where to from Here

*W*HAT TO PACK and *How to Pack* are not new questions. Adam and Eve had it easy. They just grabbed their fig leaves off the vine as they made their hasty exit from the Garden of Eden. Since then it has grown more complicated.

Hannibal, to cross the mountains, packed up his elephants. This is probably the first mention of "trunks" in history. Marco Polo's packing list must have been labor intensive. He had to plan for climate changes, take gifts for the "natives" and buy souvenirs for the folks back home. Since he didn't have a credit card, he had to carry enough cash to pay for unexpected emergencies. He, like Columbus, didn't even know where he was headed.

Phineas Fogg took two shirts, three pairs of socks and $20,000 for his trip around the world in 80 days. That approach would work today, but travelers checks and a credit card would be safer than all that cash.

Today the major problem of packing is probably that there are too many choices.

The choice of luggage types is dazzling. You may choose to travel with a suitcase, an overnighter, a duffel bag, a pullman bag, a satchel, a footlocker, a sea bag, a hanging bag, a trunk, a hat box, a train case, a soft-side — the list is almost endless.

Add to this the choice of transportation. You may travel by car, by canoe, by train, by plane, by freighter, by ship, by raft, on horseback, by dog sled, and of course, by shanks' pony.

(To this add the "emotional baggage" some people carry along and it can be quite a load. But we won't be dealing with that in this book.)

Deciding *What to Pack* begins with planning where you're going. Once you've decided on your destination, your packing is half done. The object of travelling is to leave point A with enough clothes to have a good time at destination B.

The inherent difficulties are:

1. Lifting the suitcase. The sin of taking too much has its own built-in punishment. Your arms are sore upon arrival at the tennis clinic.

2. Getting your clothes there. Thanks to the airlines, some of our luggage has seen corners of the world we can't afford to visit.

3. Being able to wear your clothes once you arrive. Do they require one vacation day to get them back into shape?

4. Leaving your room to mingle with the other guests and finding that the summer wardrobe you brought is out of place because everyone is dressed in fall colors.

5. Discovering that it's colder or warmer than you expected; you think you'll probably be sick.

This book will help you decide *What to Pack* and tell you *How to Pack* it. With its help you can look forward to packing it in and taking it on the road, with ease.

WHERE IN THE WORLD ARE YOU GOING?

A destination in a cold climate means more layers worn at once.
A warm climate requires clothes made of fabrics that breathe.
If your trip involves two climate zones, just adjust the layers.

HOW LONG ARE YOU STAYING?

Once the destination is fixed, decide how long the trip will be.
A two-week vacation doesn't require twice the clothes for one
week, but the same clothes, washed and re-arranged. A weekend
trip may require as many clothes as some week-long trips.

HOW ARE YOU GETTING THERE?

With the destination and length of the trip determined, the
mode of transportation determines what type of luggage you
take. For a boat or a yacht, the bags must fold flat. For a cruise
ship you may fill a trunk. If the safari requires you to travel by
small plane, then 22 lbs. is all you're allowed.

It gets simpler the more precisely you define the travel plans.
Before you go shopping for luggage, make certain you have some
idea of what sort of travelling you'll be doing.

The following list should get you thinking about your
packing needs.

Are you a frequent flyer on commercial airlines? If
so, use hard, foam-cast suitcases. These can take the
bumps and knocks of baggage handling. Never check
fine leather luggage. If you do see it again, it will
have more scratches than you can suffer to behold.

Do you fly away for weekend adventures? Learn to
pack a soft-sided carry-on bag. If your checked
luggage gets lost, the weekend may be over before
your bag ever arrives.

- Do you jump in your car on Friday for a weekend getaway? Yes, cardboard boxes and plastic sacks will do, but you may also buy any luggage that catches your eye. The trunk space of your car is the only limitation on what you can take. No passengers? Fill the back seat too.

- If your best friend has a sailing yacht, then a duffel bag is all you need.

- You're heading out west for a week at a ranch, and you've booked a sleeper and a seat on the train. As long as you can lift it to swing it into the rack above your head, the choice of bag is yours.

- If your travel plans are six days/six cities, take fewer clothes. Less luggage means more mobility, and only you know the outfits are repeats.

You get the picture. What you need to know before you can pack is where you are going, how long you are staying and how you are going to get there.

The Art of Packing:
Take it or Leave it

*P*ACKING is a succession of simple procedures.
How to begin?

DETERMINE THE DESTINATION.

Is it a European ski vacation or a student-with-a-backpack trip, a
budget saver, a whirlwind tour, a family visit, a camping trip, or a
no-holds-barred gala Event. (In this case you can never take too
much.)

If this is an invitation event, ask your host or hostess what
else will be going on. If you are invited to their mountain hide-
away, will there be hiking, cross country skiing or reading by the
fire? If you are invited to the seashore, does everyone fish?
Should you bring hip boots and a rod? You need to know. Ask.

DETERMINE THE LENGTH OF THE TRIP.

You can pack the same quantity of clothes for seven days of travel
as for fourteen, if you launder them once. No need to pack
double.

DETERMINE THE TYPE OF TRANSPORTATION
YOU WILL BE USING.

Are you flying to Europe, and carrying your own luggage? Will
you be driving across the States in your car, camping as you go?
Or are you going on safari in small private planes?

HOW TO USE THIS BOOK?

1. Read the table of contents and choose your destination.

2. Find the appropriate packing list under *Section I What to Pack.*

3. The icons at the side of the packing list suggest:

   a. the number of days planned for the trip;

   b. whether it is a list for men or women;

   c. how many times you need to wash your shirts, underwear and socks;

Lay the book open to the packing list, someplace where you'll see it daily. As you assemble the items in a separate place — an unused closet, an empty room, a corner — check them off the list. Write in the personal items you added that were not on the list. You don't need a new wardrobe to match each list. The lists suggest what others are most likely to be wearing and allows you to choose, from what you have, the items that best match these guidelines.

If you are travelling with someone, consider the pros and cons of sharing luggage space. Don't take doubles of things you can share — toothpaste, shampoo, sunscreen etc.

Now that you've decided *What to Pack*, you can proceed with *How to Pack – Section II.*

How to Pack explains the assortment of luggage available to you for purchase and use. Each piece of luggage has a description *How to Pack* it.

How to Pack lists the cosmetics to include in your toiletry kit. One checklist is for men, the other for women. If your cosmetics need to be revised to adapt to a destination, it is suggested at the beginning of the packing list.

How to Pack also details what you always want to have with you, by your side, on your person, in your carry-on bag.

Armed with this information, gather your things together and pack your bags.

When you return from your travels, this book will be where you left it. Before you unpack, modify the list to suit your personal élan based on the experiences you have just had.

Pre-Travel Preparations describes other elements of travel besides clothes and suitcases, mainly your passport and visas.

Transportation Options describes how to make the transportation option you choose meet your requirements.

Taking care of the home front tells you exactly how to leave a secure house so that you won't worry when you are so far away from home.

Address for information lists addresses that might be helpful to you in making your travel plans.

Publications lists are handy travel aids.

Books lists but a few of the many books available, to spur your interest in your chosen destination.

Icon Descriptions

TOILETRY KIT

Check list for each trip. If travelling together, consider doubling up on matching items from list. Lists are on page 187 for men and 189 for women. Add or delete items as list suggests.

LIST AND HINTS

☐   Open box: check off when you pack it

▩   Closed box: hint or suggestion, you choose

ICONS

Keeps you on the right page, working off the correct list. Corresponds to list in Table of Contents

Length of trip in days

List for men

List for women

List for men and women. Double the items if two people are using the same list. A blazer jacket, slacks, shirts, are suitable for men and women. The list makes it clear as to the use.

List for children

List for babies

Suggested number of times to wash underwear and socks while away.

Free Advice

*I*F YOU'RE UNDER 35 you can dress more casually and take fewer clothes. If you're over 35 and travelling abroad, you should leave the jeans at home. If you simply can't bear to do that, then always wear them with a blazer jacket. This goes for him *and* her.

If only one outfit allowed, make it a shirt, skirt, jacket, scarf, and flat leather shoes for her; long-sleeved shirt, dark slacks and jacket — with a tie folded in his pocket — and leather shoes for a man.

The person in the museum wearing sweats and running shoes is almost certainly an American tourist. If you want to look like a tourist, wear shorts on city streets. By the same token, the person wearing sandals with socks is *not* American.

You are a tourist. It *is* their country. Try to do it their way. Read up in advance on the culture you're going to be visiting. And don't forget that children need to read up on where they're going too. Get them books geared to their age level.

Try to avoid making comparisons to things back home. Enjoy the local quirks. Be open to learning something new.

Avoid rush hour if you're using public transportation. Try not to be in a hurry even when you're trying to get somewhere. It's been said before but it's still true: if someone doesn't speak English, shouting louder does not improve comprehension.

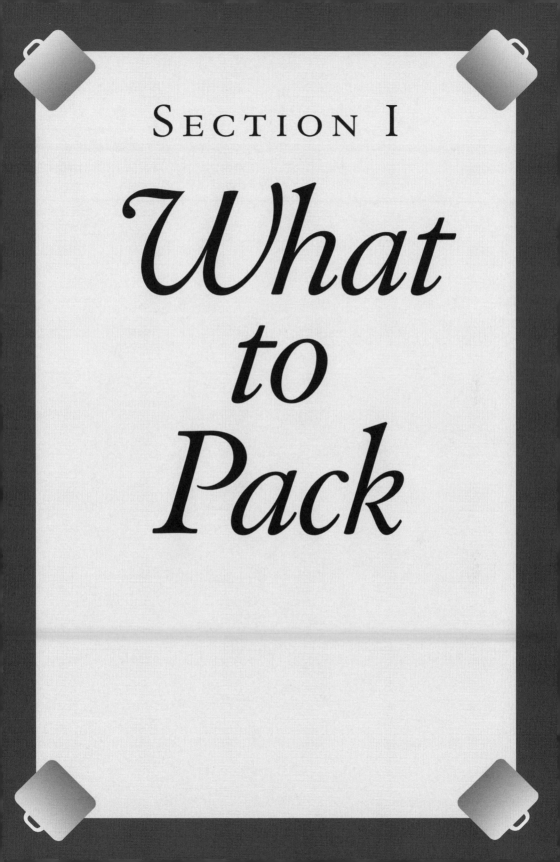

SECTION I

What to Pack

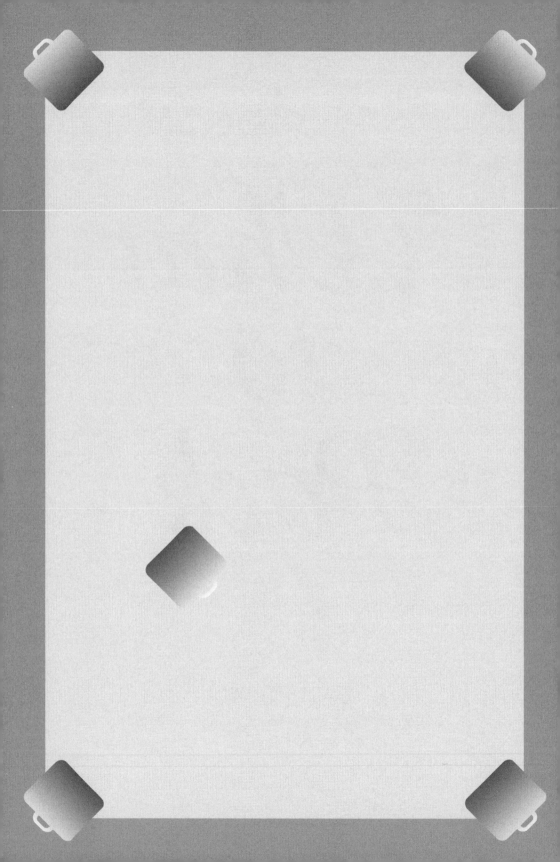

PART 1

What to Pack

for
Tours

WITH TRAVEL TIME OF
7 DAYS OR LONGER

Metropolitan Cities of the World: Men

PART 1.1

Toiletry Kit

☐ Toiletry Kit — *see How to Pack Toiletry Kit — page 187*

Clothes List

☐ Blazer jacket — solid color, preferably navy or subtle pattern

☐ 2 belts

☐ Coat — wool for winter. Lightweight raincoat for all other seasons

OR ☐ Lightweight casual outerwear jacket

☐ 1 pr cufflinks if dress shirts are French cuff

☐ 3 jeans — if you must

OR ☐ 4 slacks — cords/wool — in navy, grey or solid color for winter. (Cotton slacks in beige or other subtle colors for other seasons.) Gray — any time of year

DAYS 14

☐ 6 shirts

 ☐ 2 dress shirts — short sleeve in summer

 ☐ 2 cotton

 ☐ 2 cotton knit

☐ Shoes

 ☐ slippers/thongs/health sandals optional

 ☐ comfortable leather walking: dark leather/winter

WASH 1x7

 ☐ running shoes — just maybe for summer touring

☐ 2 pr shorts — not to be worn sightseeing, only for the seashore

☐ Sleepwear/T-shirt

☐ 5 pr socks

☐ 2 sweaters

☐ 1 swim suit — any kind

☐ 4 ties

☐ skip the umbrella, and take a crushable hat. You'll need it in London any season and on the Continent any season except in the summer

☐ 5 underwear

OPTIONAL

☐ 1 knock-about outfit for resting in hotel room can be sweats or over sized T-shirt, whatever is comfortable.

HINTS

■ Hotels offer next-afternoon laundry service if you take clothes for cleaning to the front desk at breakfast time. If you take them to a "local" cleaners or laundry you are asked to pay when bringing clothes, not when picking them up. Be certain you understand when they will be ready for pick up.

■ Wash socks and underwear in sink. If leaving the next day and they didn't dry, pack wet clothes in plastic and hang up to dry at next stop. Don't pinch a towel. Hotels keep inventory and will charge your credit card.

■ If travelling in the winter months to winter climates, substitute all short-sleeve items with long-sleeved. Eliminate cotton and pack items made of corduroy and/or wool.

Metropolitan Cities of the World: Women

PART
1.²

TOILETRY KIT

☐ Toiletry Kit — *see How to Pack Toiletry Kit* — *page 189*

CLOTHES LIST

☐ 2 belts

☐ 6 blouses or tops — camisoles for summer are fine

☐ 1 dress

☐ 1 jacket or sweater complementary to dress

☐ Coat — wool for winter. Lightweight raincoat for all other seasons

OR ☐ Light weight casual outerwear jacket

☐ Pantyhose and/or socks

☐ Shoes

    ☐ dress shoes

    ☐ comfortable walking shoes

    ☐ slippers/thongs/health sandals optional

    ☐ sport — tennis/canvas

DAYS
14

☐ 4 skirts

OR ☐ 4 dresses

☐ 2 pr slacks

OR ☐ 4 pr of slacks and 2 skirts

WASH
1 x 7

OR ☐ 4 pr shorts — Bermuda length for summer in place of slacks and leggings (if in fashion)

- [ ] 3 sweaters
- [ ] 1 swimsuit
- [ ] 1 sleepwear/T-shirt
- [ ] 5 underwear
- [ ] Small dress purse optional
- [ ] Large tote bag — counts as purse
- [ ] Gloves — a must in fall and winter
- [ ] Scarf for coat — wool in winter — *see Religious Sites, page 30*
- [ ] skip the umbrella, and take a crushable hat

HINTS

Hotels offer next-afternoon laundry service if you take clothes for cleaning to the front desk at breakfast time. If you take them to a "local" cleaners or laundry you are asked to pay when bringing clothes, not when picking them up. Be certain you understand when they will be ready for pick up.

Wash socks and underwear in sink. If leaving the next day and they didn't dry, pack wet clothes in plastic and hang up to dry at next stop. Don't pinch a towel. Hotels keep inventory and will charge your credit card.

If travelling in the winter months to winter climates, substitute all short-sleeve items with long-sleeved. Eliminate cotton and pack items made of corduroy and/or wool.

Religious Holy Sites and Shrines

PART 1.³

☐ Wear a light weight shawl or scarf to cover your upper body when entering churches and cathedrals, even if only to view the art.

☐ Shoes must be removed at some sites because small heels damage the floors.

☐ No shorts. No skimpy tops.

☐ *Do not* allow children to run loose or make noise — a service may be in progress.

☐ *Do* donate money in appreciation.

Metropolitan Cities of the World: Students

DEFINITION OF STUDENT

- [ ] Anyone who wears only jeans, has no kids in tow and carries everything in a backpack. No money.

- [ ] *This is a "bare bones" list and includes cosmetics.*

BACKPACK

- [ ] Backpack and small duffle bag will take the following:
  - [ ] Address book and pen
  - [ ] Baseball cap
  - [ ] 1 belt — wear it
  - [ ] Camera and film
  - [ ] 1 jacket — denim/leather/you-name-it
  - [ ] 3 pr jeans — wear one pair
  - [ ] Plastic rain poncho
  - [ ] 5 T-shirts
  - [ ] 5 boxer shorts — these double as swimsuit, sleepwear and underwear for boys. Girls adjust accordingly
- [ ] Shoes
  - [ ] running shoes
  - [ ] thongs/sandals/shoes
- [ ] 4 pr socks — if you wear socks

PART
1.⁴

CONTINUED

- [ ] 2 sweatshirts — with logo, sayings, faces etc. (definitely not plain)
- [ ] Swimsuit — girls
- [ ] 1 Swiss army knife
- [ ] 1 towel
- [ ] Blemish-control creme
- [ ] Comb/brush
- [ ] Deodorant (if you forget it, you'll fit in fine in some countries anyway)
- [ ] Toothbrush
- [ ] Toothpaste
- [ ] Shampoo/soap
- [ ] Shaver
- [ ] Sunscreen

HINTS

- [ ] Take some of your money in travelers checks. Leave a copy of the numbers at home. Take a credit card too, but guard it.

- [ ] Arrange for a *USA Direct* card. Memorize the number and guard it when you use it.

- [ ] Don't leave your passport anywhere you're not. Campgrounds and hostels have safes at the reception area where you check your "valuables." Do it. Your passport is a valuable.

- [ ] Put your name and address on your bags in ink.

- [ ] Jeans are good for wearing, currency, exchanging, making acquaintances, and for sleeping.

▪ Put exposed film at the bottom of the bag.
If you "lose" your camera, your memories will
make it home.

▪ If you're part of a group travelling together, don't
go to sleep on the trains unless one of you stays
awake. Someone needs to guard the luggage.
If you all sleep, it is all likely to be gone when
you awake. If travelling alone on the train,
sleep some other time.

Cruises: Warm Climate

PART
1.⁵

Not to Pack: jeans, polyester anything, rayon (does not breathe as well as silks and cotton)

TOILETRY KIT

Toiletry Kit — *see How To Pack Toiletry Kit — page 187-189*

CLOTHES LIST

- 3 belts
- 4 dresses — sheaths are great for dinners

OR
- 4 skirts and blouses
- Hats — cotton/straw/visor
- 6 shirts — cotton/linen, solid/light-striped —M
- 4 shorts — not short shorts —M —W
- 4 tops — coordinated
- 4 slacks — navy/white/solids - M
- 2 jackets
- Jewelry — *Show time!* earrings/bracelets/necklaces cufflinks for French cuffed shirts
- 1 jogging suit/leisure sportswear
- 4 pr shoes
  - classic leather sandal
  - canvas shoe

DAYS
7

WASH
0

☐ dress for evening
☐ sports
☐ 3 lightweight sweaters
☐ 3 swimsuits
☐ 1 swimsuit cover-up — long shirt/jumpsuit
☐ 2 cocktail dresses
Or ☐ 1 dress skirt and 2 evening tops
☐ 1 tux plus shirt/studs/cummerbund/tie —M
☐ Scarves/shawls
☐ Sleepwear
☐ 7 pr socks
☐ 6 ties —M
☐ 7 underwear

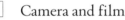

PART
1.⁵

EQUIPMENT

☐ Camera and film

HINTS

▪ Ask your travel arranger for advance information on the cruise. You want to know the following:
   How many black tie dinners?
   Any other dress codes?
   What is the onboard entertainment?
   What sports are played onboard?
   Is there a library onboard? Even so, bring
      reading material.

▪ Once onboard, it is not so easy to get what you want. Being on a cruise is like living in a town with limited supplies. Purchases onboard will not be a bargain.

▪ If you already own the clothes described in the list, take them by all means, but know that many of your fellow passengers have bought all new clothes

PART

1.⁵

CONTINUED

especially for the trip. Your old favorite, in the light and glare of new all around you, might look tired and make you feel uncomfortable.

☐ Shawls and scarves create new looks for evening. One basic sheath dress can go a long way.

☐ Clothes may be any colors the hotter the weather, the brighter the colors. There will be lots of white, navy, gold and primary colors. Designs you will see: lots of fish, flowers, shells and nautical. Better-dressed women wear more skirts than shorts.

☐ Better-dressed men wear slacks and blazers.

☐ Materials: all natural - cotton, linen, silk.

Cruises: Deluxe

Not to Pack: jeans, polyester anything, rayon (does not breathe as well as silks and cotton). The Western ranch look/country clothes/seaside attire will not be appropriate.

TOILETRY KIT

☐ Toiletry Kit - *see How To Pack Toiletry Kit — page 187-189*

CLOTHES LIST

☐ 3 belts

☐ 6 dresses — sheaths are great for dinners

OR ☐ 4 skirts/blouses — more for afternoon tea

☐ Hats — cotton/straw/visor

☐ 6 shirts — cotton/linen, solid/light-striped —M

☐ 6 shorts — not short shorts —M —W

☐ 6 tops — coordinated

☐ 6 slacks — navy/white/solids —M

☐ 4 jackets

☐ Jewelry - *Show Time!* earrings/bracelets/necklaces, cuff links for French cuff shirts

☐ 2 jogging suits/leisure sportswear

☐ 6 pr shoes

  ☐ classic leather sandal

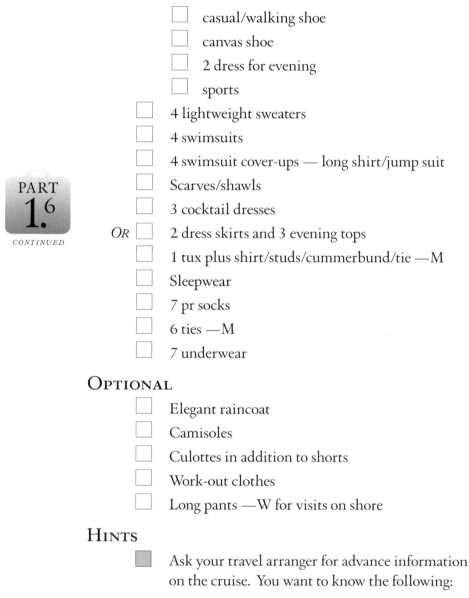

- [ ] casual/walking shoe
- [ ] canvas shoe
- [ ] 2 dress for evening
- [ ] sports
- [ ] 4 lightweight sweaters
- [ ] 4 swimsuits
- [ ] 4 swimsuit cover-ups — long shirt/jump suit
- [ ] Scarves/shawls
- [ ] 3 cocktail dresses

OR

- [ ] 2 dress skirts and 3 evening tops
- [ ] 1 tux plus shirt/studs/cummerbund/tie —M
- [ ] Sleepwear
- [ ] 7 pr socks
- [ ] 6 ties —M
- [ ] 7 underwear

PART
1.⁶

CONTINUED

OPTIONAL

- [ ] Elegant raincoat
- [ ] Camisoles
- [ ] Culottes in addition to shorts
- [ ] Work-out clothes
- [ ] Long pants —W for visits on shore

HINTS

Ask your travel arranger for advance information on the cruise. You want to know the following:

How many black tie dinners?
Any other dress codes?
What is the onboard entertainment?
What sports are played onboard
Is there a library on board? Even so, bring reading material.

☐ Once onboard, it is not so easy to get what you want. Being on a cruise is like living in a town with limited supplies.

☐ If you already own the clothes described in the list, take them by all means, but know that many of your fellow passengers have bought all new clothes especially for the trip. Your old favorite, in the light and glare of new all around you, might look tired and make you feel uncomfortable.

PART

1.⁶

☐ Shawls and scarves create new looks for evening. Two or three basic sheath dresses go a long way. Plan six days of no repeat items.

☐ Clothes may be any colors the hotter the weather, the brighter the colors. There will be lots of white, navy, gold and primary colors. Designs you will see: lots of fish, flowers, shells and nautical. Better-dressed women wear more skirts than shorts during the day. Sport clothes will be chic, smart, and everyone will have lots of them.

☐ Fine jewelry will be more in abundance.

☐ Better-dressed men wear slacks and blazers during the day.

☐ Materials: all natural: cotton, linen, silk.

Cruises: Cold Climate

PART
1.⁷

□ *Not to pack:* polyester or rayon

TOILETRY KIT

□ Toiletry Kit - *see How To Pack Toiletry Kit — page 187-189*

CLOTHES LIST

□ Bandannas or scarves for head and neck

□ 1 pr knee-high rubber boots

□ 2 hats: one for sun, one for warmth

□ 3 dresses —W

OR □ 3 skirts and top

□ 3 pr slacks —M

□ 3 dress shirts —M

□ 3 pr pants — jeans ok

□ 3 wool shirts

□ 2 pr shorts — on the chance that weather turns warm

□ 3 sweaters

OR □ 2 sweatshirts

□ 3 long-sleeve turtleneck shirts

□ 2 windbreakers

OR □ 1 set of rain gear

□ Shoes

DAYS
7

WASH
0

☐ 2 pr shoes — tie-on, rubber-soled shoes
with tread i.e. canvas/deck

☐ tennis shoes/athletic shoes

☐ 1 pr dress shoes — flat-heeled

☐ Sleepwear — flannel

☐ Sunglasses

☐ 6 pr socks

☐ 2 ties

☐ Underwear

PART
1.7

EQUIPMENT

☐ Binoculars — a must

☐ Camera and film

☐ Flashlight

☐ 1 pr spare eyeglasses (if applicable)

HINTS

Since this is a cruise to the north, ie. Alaska, Norway
or colder climates, you need to think about warmth.
Pack clothes that can be worn in layers. It will be
cold when passing glaciers. Shirt sleeves alone will
never be enough.

In addition to the uncommon sights, dinner is also an
event, and most guests dress for dinner.

Most ships provide a robe for use in the cabin.

The smaller the ship, the bigger the requirement for
soft luggage. Ask about the size.

Once onboard, it is not easy to purchase extra things.
Being on a cruise is like living in a town with limited
supplies. Purchases onboard will not be a bargain.

The passengers will be interested in the outdoors more
than might be the case on a cruise in the warm climates.
The boots are for discovery excursions on shore.

Cruises: Small Yacht
Exotic Destination:
South Pacific; Greek Islands

PART
1.⁸

All space is limited, so pack accordingly. Clothes will be scrunched. Pack a duffle bag and store it under your mattress. Hang space is limited.

TOILETRY KIT

- [ ] Toiletry Kit - *see How To Pack Toiletry Kit — page 187-189*
- [ ] Amend toiletry kit to take only travel/sample size, as head (wc) and shower — if there is one — are compact
- [ ] Motion-sickness medication
- [ ] Sunblock in addition to sunscreen
- [ ] More sunscreen

CLOTHES LIST

DAYS
7

- [ ] 1 long pants
- [ ] 2 pr shorts
- [ ] 4 pr socks
- [ ] 2 pr shoes — tie-on, rubber-soled shoes with tread i.e. canvas/deck/running/tennis shoes
  - [ ] Sandals for shore visits
  - [ ] Shoes for beachcombing
- [ ] Sleepwear

WASH
0

- [ ] 1 sweater
- [ ] Swimsuit for each day, this is what you live in

- ☐ 3 tank tops
- ☐ 2 short-sleeved T-shirts
- ☐ Underwear
- ☐ Visor
- ☐ Windbreaker — lightweight, waterproof, bright-colored
- ☐ Cover-up wraps for swimsuit to walk on shore

EQUIPMENT

- ☐ Camera and film
- ☐ Sunglasses

HINTS

☐ No metal watchbands or bracelets. Check all clothes and jewelry for anything that could scratch the varnish.

☐ You will be living in your swimsuit, but it is not appropriate attire for excursions ashore. Long lengths of fabric that make "island dresses" are good cover-ups.

☐ The captain of the boat has the final word. Don't tell him when to sail. Don't tell him how or where to sail. Don't tell him your romantic problems. Don't party with his crew. Don't book for more than two weeks. This is really confined space!

Disneyland: Low Budget

☐ This example is included to suggest that you can have a great vacation with little luggage.

TOILETRY KIT

☐ Toiletry Kit - *see How To Pack Toiletry Kit — page 187-189.* Adjust to minimal

☐ Travel-size shampoo — not supplied at budget-rate lodgings

☐ Plastic bag for swimsuit

☐ Sunscreen — highest number for protection. Cheaper to buy at home before travelling

CLOTHES LIST

☐ Hat or visor for sun

☐ 1 lightweight jacket

☐ 2 pr shorts - cotton

☐ 3 T-shirts

☐ 1 pr good walking shoes

☐ 3 pr socks — takes up the wet from sweat

☐ 3 underpants

☐ 2 bras —W

☐ Sunglasses

☐ Swimsuit — hotel will most likely have pool

☐ Sleepwear can double as swimsuit cover

☐ Camera and extra film (cheaper to buy at home)

PART
1.⁹

DAYS
7

WASH
3x7

HINTS

- Book an inexpensive motel or hotel. They usually provide bus service to the park. Plan to eat picnic style in parks, or in your room.

- Take one duffle bag and one backpack. Pack clothes for 2 days and wash them out each night and hang them to dry in the shower. (Do not hang clothes out the window to dry — management will not be pleased if you do.)

- Use the backpack to carry your valuables in each day as you sightsee. Use it also for grocery shopping for your picnic supplies.

- Film for your camera is more expensive at Disneyland — bring extra rolls with you.

- Plastic bags are good for wet swimsuits, dirty laundry and shampoo that might spill.

- Use your hotel glasses for your picnics, or buy paper ware.

- Take your Swiss army knife. It has a bottle opener, and it cuts up the vegetables and makes picnicking easier.

PART

1.9

Resorts: Summer

PART

1.10

TOILETRY KIT

- [ ] Add to Toiletry Kit - *see How To Pack Toiletry Kit — page 187-189*
- [ ] After-sun lotion
- [ ] Antiseptic creme
- [ ] Insecticide/insect repellent
- [ ] Quinine
- [ ] Sunblock of highest number — expensive to buy there
- [ ] Sunscreen
- [ ] Zinc for nose

CLOTHES LIST

DAYS

7

- [ ] 2 belts
- [ ] Blazer or jacket — dresses up Bermuda shorts and pants for dinner —M —W
- [ ] 4 dresses for dinner

OR
- [ ] 4 skirts and tops
- [ ] 4 shorts —M —W
- [ ] 6 tops —M —W
- [ ] 4 long pants —M

WASH

1x**7**

- [ ] 1 three-foot square cotton scarf in coordinated color. Use as bodice scarf; drape over blazer; use as hair cover-up; tie around hat to keep it on during boat ride

- [ ] Sleepwear
- [ ] Shoes
  - [ ] dress shoes for evening
  - [ ] sandals
  - [ ] sport shoes for activities
- [ ] Sun hat, or buy straw hat there
- [ ] Sunglasses with dark lenses.
- [ ] 3 swimsuits, minimum. This is all-day wear — the more the merrier
- [ ] Swimsuit cover-up for lunch on terrace
- [ ] Tennis clothes — some resorts require white
- [ ] 4 ties —M
- [ ] 6 underwear

PART
1.10

SPORTS EQUIPMENT

- [x] Ask what is available
- [ ] Diving
- [ ] Golf
- [ ] Horseback riding
- [ ] Squash
- [ ] Tennis

HINTS

- [x] To this destination it is acceptable to wear leisure suits on the plane. If young, sweats are "o.k". It looks right for resorts. Select shoes accordingly.

- [x] All-cotton sleepwear. All-cotton underwear. Minimize rayon for daytime wear. Avoid polyester T-shirts, shorts or blouses. Linen is good but requires more care unless blended with percentage of synthetic fibers.

Shoes should be broken in to prevent blisters. More heat means more sweat and more rubbing.

Be prepared for well-dressed fellow travellers. Dressier than just going to the seashore for summer vacation. Dinner is a dress event in most cases. If everything mixes and matches, each part can be worn twice. Pastel colors are easy to combine, but bright colors are de règle.

PART

1.¹⁰

CONTINUED

Beach bag - woven fabric to let sand run out and to carry books, reading glasses, sunglasses, and sunscreen to the beach.

Towels for the beach are supplied by the resort.

Resorts: Winter

TOILETRY KIT

- [ ] Add to Toiletry Kit - *see How To Pack Toiletry Kit — page 187-189*
- [ ] After-sun lotion
- [ ] Antiseptic creme
- [ ] Insecticide/insect repellent
- [ ] Quinine
- [ ] Sunblock — expensive to buy there
- [ ] Sunscreen

CLOTHES LIST

- [ ] 2 belts
- [ ] 2 blazers or jackets — evenings may be cool —M —W
- [ ] 4 dresses for dinner
- OR [ ] 4 skirts and tops
- OR [ ] 4 long pants —W
- [ ] 4 Bermuda-length shorts —M —W
- [ ] 6 tops —M —W
- [ ] 4 long pants —M
- [ ] 1 three-foot square cotton scarf in coordinated color: drape over blazer; use as hair cover-up; tie around hat to keep it on in a breeze
- [ ] Jewelry

- [ ] Sleepwear
- [ ] Shoes
  - [ ] dress shoes for evening
  - [ ] sandals
  - [ ] sport shoes for activities
- [ ] 2 sweaters
- [ ] Sun hat, or buy straw hat there
- [ ] Sunglasses
- [ ] 3 swimsuits — minimum. This is all day wear - the more the merrier
- [ ] Swimsuit cover-up for lunch on terrace
- [ ] Tennis clothes — some resorts require white
- [ ] 4 ties —M
- [ ] 6 underwear

PART 1.11

CONTINUED

SPORTS EQUIPMENT

- [x] Ask what is available
- [ ] Diving
- [ ] Golf
- [ ] Horseback riding
- [ ] Squash
- [ ] Tennis

HINTS

- [x] To this destination it is acceptable to wear leisure suits on the plane. It looks right for resorts. Select shoes accordingly.

- [x] All-cotton sleepwear. All-cotton underwear. Minimize rayon for daytime wear. Linen is good but requires more care unless blended with some percentage of synthetic fibers.

☐ When you travel south in winter, the nights there might be colder than you expect.

☐ Be prepared for well-dressed fellow travellers. Dinner is a dress event. If everything mixes and matches each part can be worn twice. Bright colors are not worn as much in winter — wear fall and winter colors. Summer clothes look out-of-place. A simple flowing skirt and blouse for evening is fine. Combine with a sweater.

PART
1.11

☐ Beach bag - woven fabric to let sand run out and to carry books, reading glasses, sunglasses, and sunscreen to the beach.

☐ Towels for the beach are supplied by the resort.

PART 2

What to Pack

for
"Great Escapes"

WITH TRAVEL TIME OF
7 DAYS OR LONGER

Health Farm: Europe

PART 2.1

TOILETRY KIT

- [ ] Toiletry Kit - *see How To Pack Toiletry Kit — page 187-189*

CLOTHES LIST

- [ ] Bathrobe or terry cloth dressing gown
- [ ] Cotton headband
- [ ] 3 exercise/work-out outfits
- [ ] 2 leisure/jogging suits
- [ ] Shoes
  - [ ] training shoes or ballet slippers with ankle warmers to keep muscles warm
  - [ ] thongs or mules
  - [ ] walking shoes
- [ ] Swimsuit
- [ ] Large sweatshirt to go over exercise outfit will also go over swimsuit

DAYS 7

DINNER CLOTHES

- [ ] 3 pr slacks —M
- [ ] 3 skirts —W
- [ ] 6 shirts/blouses —M —W
- [ ] 2 belts
- [ ] 3 scarves —W
- [ ] 3 ties —M

WASH 1x7

☐ 1 jacket and 2 sweaters

OR ☐ 3 sweaters —M —W

☐ 1 pr leather shoes

☐ Sleepwear

☐ 6 pr socks

☐ 6 underwear

HINTS

☐ Washing things out by hand is only possible in a limited way — most items will have to be sent to the laundry, so don't bother with the idea of hand washing.

☐ Ask what sports are available and take the appropriate outfits.

☐ Dress depends on the "package" you book. This is not a "Farmer Brown" farm.

☐ "Diet plan" means you stay in your terry robe or dressing gown all day. "Regular plan" means dining room dress.

☐ If you plan to wear jeans to dinner, wear with blazer jacket. Europeans do. Dress may be casual for dinner, but ask at time of booking.

Olympics: Summer

PART
2.²

TOILETRY KIT

- [ ] Add to Toiletry Kit - *see How To Pack Toiletry Kit — page 187-189*
- [ ] After-sun lotion
- [ ] Sunblock of highest number
- [ ] Sunscreen
- [ ] Zinc for nose — a must

CLOTHES LIST

- [ ] 2 belts
- [ ] Blazer or jacket — dresses up Bermuda shorts and pants for dinner —M —W
- [ ] 4 skirts —W
- OR [ ] 5 Bermuda shorts —M —W
- OR [ ] 4 long pants —M
- OR [ ] 4 leisure wear outfits
- [ ] 6 tops —M —W
- [ ] Sleepwear
- [ ] Shoes — should be broken in to prevent blisters. More heat means more sweat and more rubbing. May be sport shoes if suits are leisurewear
  - [ ] Dress shoes for evening
- [ ] Sun hat or visor
- [ ] Sunglasses with dark lenses

DAYS
7

WASH
1x7

☐ Swimsuit

☐ Swimsuit cover-up

☐ Large tote bag or backpack

☐ 2 ties —M

☐ 6 underwear

HINTS

▪ To this destination it is acceptable to wear leisurewear suits on the plane. If young, sweats look right for the Olympics. Choose shoes accordingly.

▪ All-cotton sleepwear. All-cotton underwear. Minimize rayon for daytime wear. Avoid polyester T-shirts, blouses, or shorts.

▪ If everything mixes and matches, each part can be worn twice.

▪ Plan on standing or sitting most of your day watching the events. You want to wear comfortable, easy-to-care-for clothes. You aren't a participating athlete so you don't have to look like one. But, remember you do represent your country to others.

▪ You will need an over-the-shoulder tote or backpack to carry sunscreen, visor, bottle of water — whatever you need to get through the day.

Olympics: Winter

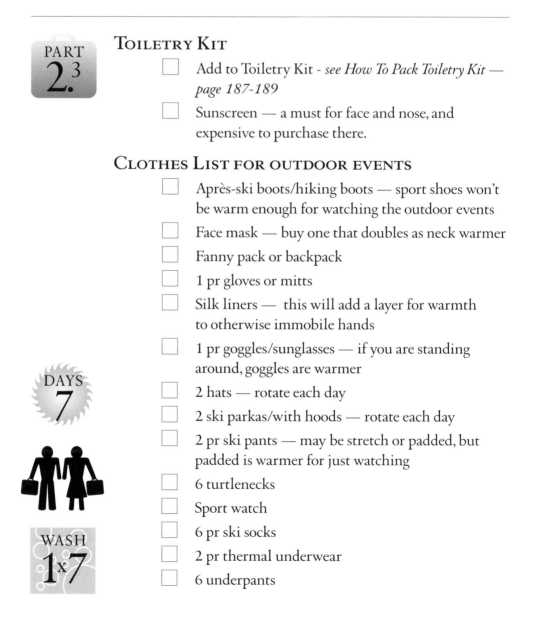

PART 2.³

TOILETRY KIT

- ☐ Add to Toiletry Kit - *see How To Pack Toiletry Kit — page 187-189*
- ☐ Sunscreen — a must for face and nose, and expensive to purchase there.

CLOTHES LIST FOR OUTDOOR EVENTS

- ☐ Après-ski boots/hiking boots — sport shoes won't be warm enough for watching the outdoor events
- ☐ Face mask — buy one that doubles as neck warmer
- ☐ Fanny pack or backpack
- ☐ 1 pr gloves or mitts
- ☐ Silk liners — this will add a layer for warmth to otherwise immobile hands
- ☐ 1 pr goggles/sunglasses — if you are standing around, goggles are warmer
- ☐ 2 hats — rotate each day
- ☐ 2 ski parkas/with hoods — rotate each day
- ☐ 2 pr ski pants — may be stretch or padded, but padded is warmer for just watching
- ☐ 6 turtlenecks
- ☐ Sport watch
- ☐ 6 pr ski socks
- ☐ 2 pr thermal underwear
- ☐ 6 underpants

DAYS 7

WASH 1x7

CLOTHES LIST FOR INDOOR EVENTS
AND EVENINGS

- ☐ 2 belts
- ☐ 1 blazer —M —W
- ☐ 3 pr jeans —M —W
- *Or* ☐ 4 pr long pants —M —W
- ☐ 2 sweaters
- *Or* ☐ 2 sweatshirts
- *Or* ☐ 3 leisure/jogging suits
- ☐ 6 turtleneck T-shirts — see list above
- ☐ 1 wool skirt and top —W
- *Or* ☐ 1 wool dressy outfit —W
- ☐ Shoes
    - ☐ dress shoes for evening
    - ☐ sport shoes for indoors
- ☐ Sleepwear — flannel
- ☐ Slippers — floors might be cold and bathroom may be down the hall
- ☐ 2 ties —M

HINTS

☐ To this destination it is acceptable to wear leisure/jogging suits on the plane. It looks right for the Olympics. Select shoes accordingly.

☐ If everything mixes and matches, each part can be worn twice. Bright colors for evening wear are not worn as much in winter — wear fall and winter colors. Summer clothes look out-of-place. The dressy outfit is for that special dinner out.

☐ The fanny pack or backpack is in lieu of a purse to carry around the things you need all day, including your room keys, Kleenex and your sunscreen.

Ranch Vacation

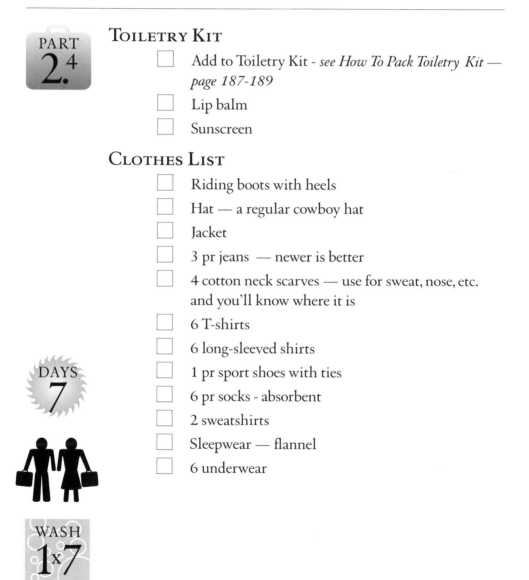

PART 2.⁴

TOILETRY KIT

- [ ] Add to Toiletry Kit - *see How To Pack Toiletry Kit — page 187-189*
- [ ] Lip balm
- [ ] Sunscreen

CLOTHES LIST

- [ ] Riding boots with heels
- [ ] Hat — a regular cowboy hat
- [ ] Jacket
- [ ] 3 pr jeans — newer is better
- [ ] 4 cotton neck scarves — use for sweat, nose, etc. and you'll know where it is
- [ ] 6 T-shirts
- [ ] 6 long-sleeved shirts
- [ ] 1 pr sport shoes with ties
- [ ] 6 pr socks - absorbent
- [ ] 2 sweatshirts
- [ ] Sleepwear — flannel
- [ ] 6 underwear

DAYS **7**

WASH **1x7**

HINTS

- Now you can buy and wear all those "Western clothes" that look silly anywhere else in the US.

- Wear your jeans over your boots, not tucked in your boots.

- Cowboys dress like you see them at the ranch. It is not a fashion statement.

Safari

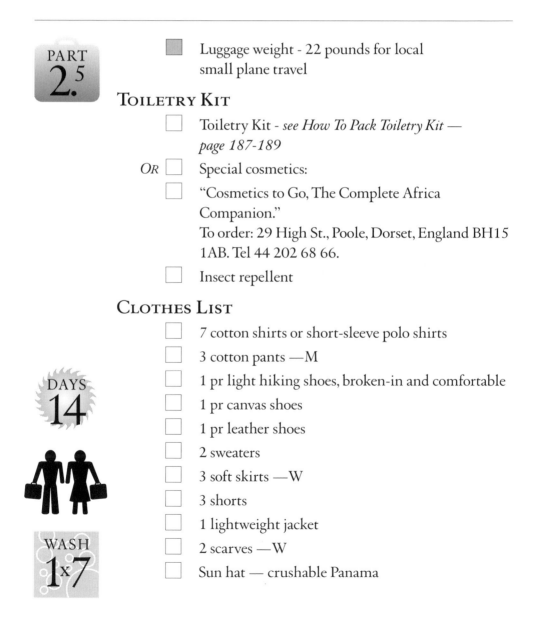

PART 2.⁵

▣ Luggage weight - 22 pounds for local small plane travel

TOILETRY KIT

☐ Toiletry Kit - *see How To Pack Toiletry Kit — page 187-189*

OR ☐ Special cosmetics:

☐ "Cosmetics to Go, The Complete Africa Companion."
To order: 29 High St., Poole, Dorset, England BH15 1AB. Tel 44 202 68 66.

☐ Insect repellent

CLOTHES LIST

☐ 7 cotton shirts or short-sleeve polo shirts

☐ 3 cotton pants —M

☐ 1 pr light hiking shoes, broken-in and comfortable

☐ 1 pr canvas shoes

☐ 1 pr leather shoes

☐ 2 sweaters

☐ 3 soft skirts —W

☐ 3 shorts

☐ 1 lightweight jacket

☐ 2 scarves —W

☐ Sun hat — crushable Panama

DAYS 14

WASH 1x7

☐   2 sleepwear

☐   7 underwear

☐   7 pr socks

EQUIPMENT

☐   Wide-angle binoculars, not pocket type

☐   Quiet camera and lots of film!

HINTS

PART
2.5

☐   Wear earth tones, beige or brown. Avoid white.

☐   Consider buying zip-off pants that convert to shorts. A "travellers" vest has many pockets — some with zippers or velcro closing — leaves hands free and eliminates the need for a fanny pack or an over-the-shoulder bag.

☐   Dinners may be elegant and in large tents.

☐   On a safari, the goal is to view nature and visitors should blend in. The animals are the center of attraction.

Spa:
Fall, Winter, Spring

PART 2.⁶

☐ In the *Summer* take less outerwear

TOILETRY KIT

☐ Add to Toiletry Kit - *see How To Pack Toiletry Kit — page 187-189.* Pack minimal make-up

☐ Shampoo/conditioner are supplied

☐ Lip balm

☐ Sunscreen

CLOTHES LIST

☐ 3 jogging bras —W

☐ 3 lycra exercise shorts

☐ Fanny pack or backpack to carry room key

☐ Glasses

☐ Gloves for morning hike

☐ Hat

☐ 3 leggings and 4 tops

OR ☐ 3 pr slacks and 3 sweaters

OR ☐ 3 pr jeans and 4 shirts, depending on your style

☐ 2 lycra long running pants

☐ 2 warm-up/leisure suits — for casual dress, not work out

DAYS 7

WASH 0

- [ ] Shoes
  - [ ] 1 pr cross trainers
  - [ ] 1 pr light hiking boots
  - [ ] 1 pr loafers
- [ ] 5 T-shirts
- [ ] 2 turtlenecks
- [ ] Sleepwear
- [ ] 8 pr socks — light and heavy
- [ ] Swimsuit
- [ ] 2 sweatshirt
- [ ] 6 underwear
- [ ] Watch
- [ ] Windbreaker — lightweight with pockets

PART
2.6

HINTS

- Purchase sweat clothes or towel with the logo there.

- Take a supply of books and magazines.

- Leave your jewelry at home.

Yoga Retreat

PART
2.⁷

■ Read information sent by retreat organizers

TOILETRY KIT

☐ Toiletry Kit - *see How To Pack Toiletry Kit — page 187-189.* Adjust to minimal

CLOTHES LIST

☐ Scarves —large and flowing
☐ Shawl for meditation
☐ Shoes
    ☐ canvas or walking
    ☐ sandals/thongs
☐ 4 shorts
☐ 6 T-shirts
☐ 2 skirts
☐ Sleepwear
☐ Sweatpants
☐ Sweatshirt
☐ Swimsuit
☐ Swimsuit cover-up
☐ 6 underwear
☐ Windbreaker or rainwear

DAYS
7

EQUIPMENT

☐ Bath towel

WASH
2x7

- [ ] Washcloth
- [ ] Beach towel
- [ ] Camera and film
- [ ] Notebook
- [ ] Pens/pencils
- [ ] Pillow if needed
- [ ] Sleeping bag or 2 sheets and blanket
- [ ] Soap in plastic container
- [ ] Textbooks
- [ ] Yoga mat

PART
2.⁷

HINTS

When reserving a space at the retreat, ask the total number of guests that are expected your week and how many are assigned to sleep in your room with you.

Ask about the weather and the season of the year. If it is not summer, add long pants and a sweater to the list.

Adjust your wardrobe needs to the location of the retreat. Is it at the seashore or in the mountains?

If this is a work retreat, add a pair of jeans and two T-shirts.

All clothes should be loose fitting.

What to Pack

for Sports Vacations

WITH TRAVEL TIME OF
7 DAYS OR LONGER

Biking: Summer

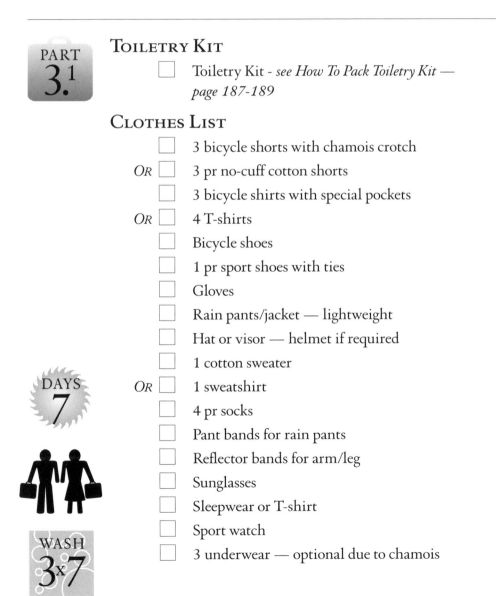

PART 3.1

TOILETRY KIT

☐ Toiletry Kit - *see How To Pack Toiletry Kit —* *page 187-189*

CLOTHES LIST

☐ 3 bicycle shorts with chamois crotch

OR ☐ 3 pr no-cuff cotton shorts

☐ 3 bicycle shirts with special pockets

OR ☐ 4 T-shirts

☐ Bicycle shoes

☐ 1 pr sport shoes with ties

☐ Gloves

☐ Rain pants/jacket — lightweight

☐ Hat or visor — helmet if required

☐ 1 cotton sweater

OR ☐ 1 sweatshirt

☐ 4 pr socks

☐ Pant bands for rain pants

☐ Reflector bands for arm/leg

☐ Sunglasses

☐ Sleepwear or T-shirt

☐ Sport watch

☐ 3 underwear — optional due to chamois

DAYS 7

WASH 3x7

HINTS

■ Wear one pair of bicycle shorts and one bicycle shirt or one pair of no-cuff cotton shorts and T-shirt while travelling to your starting destination. Wear sport shoes with ties.

■ Ask if trip requires any other style of dress than this:

☐ 1 pr dress Bermuda shorts

☐ 2 cotton shirts

☐ 1 cotton sweater

☐ 1 pr casual shoes — light canvas, no socks needed

EQUIPMENT

☐ Camera and film

Biking:
Fall and Spring

PART
3.²

Toiletry Kit

☐ Toiletry Kit — *see How to Pack Toiletry Kit —*
page 187-189

Clothes List

☐ 3 pr long lycra pants

OR ☐ 3 pr no-cuff cotton long pants

☐ 3 bicycle shirts with special pockets

OR ☐ 4 turtleneck shirts

☐ Bicycle shoes

☐ 1 pr sport shoes with ties

☐ Gloves

☐ Rain pants/jacket — lightweight

☐ Hat or visor — helmet if required

☐ 1 sweater

OR ☐ 1 sweatshirt

☐ 1 sweatpants

☐ 4 pr socks

☐ Pant bands

☐ Reflector bands for arm/leg

☐ Sport watch

☐ Sunglasses

☐ Sleepwear or T-shirt

☐ 4 underwear

DAYS
7

WASH
3ₓ7

HINTS

- ▨ Ask if trip requires any other style of dress:
- ☐ 1 pr dresspants —M /skirt —W
- ☐ 2 cotton shirts/blouses —M —W
- ☐ Sweater
- ☐ 1 pr casual leather shoes

EQUIPMENT

- ☐ Camera and film

Biking: Bicycle Touring

PART
3.³

BICYCLE PACKING LIST

- [ ] Bicycle — add soft-seat
- [ ] Saddle bags for rear of bike
- [ ] Handlebar bag with map compartment
- [ ] Bell
- [ ] Bicycle cover for rain optional
- [ ] Bicycle lock
- [ ] Bicycle pump
- [ ] Stretch bands
- [ ] Repair kit for tires
- [ ] Stretch bands for securing luggage
- [ ] Extra tube for tire — if required
- [ ] Water bottle and rack

EQUIPMENT

- [ ] Camera and film

HINTS/BICYCLE TIPS

- [x] Learn basic bicycle repair
- [x] Learn basic first-aid
- [x] Learn rules-of-the-road and traffic signs
- [x] Practice before going — a saddle sore seat makes for a miserable trip

Camping: Tent

TOILETRY KIT

☐ Add to Toiletry Kit - *see How To Pack Toiletry Kit — page 187-189*

☐ First-aid kit

☐ Insect repellent

☐ Sunblock of highest number

☐ Zinc for nose

CLOTHES LIST

☐ 1 belt

☐ 2 pr jeans

☐ 2 pr shorts

☐ 4 T-shirts

☐ 1 long-sleeved shirt

☐ 1 set of rain gear

☐ Walking shoes

☐ Hiking boots

☐ 5 pr socks

☐ 2 sweatshirts

☐ Sunglasses

☐ Underwear

EQUIPMENT

☐ Backpack

PART
3.4
CONTINUED

- ☐ Bed roll/sleeping bag
- ☐ Camping plate/cup/bowl
- ☐ Camping knife/fork/spoon
- ☐ Camping stove
- ☐ Cooking utensils
- ☐ First aid kit —if not added to toiletry kit
- ☐ Flashlight
- ☐ Food — dried
- ☐ Detailed map of the area
- ☐ Matches
- ☐ Plastic garbage bags
- ☐ Plastic milk jug — gallon size
- ☐ Rope
- ☐ Swiss army knife
- ☐ Tent
- ☐ Toilet paper
- ☐ Towels

HINTS

- ▨ Backpack must be comfortable.
- ▨ You change your clothes when they are wet, not because they are dirty.
- ▨ If it rains while trekking, put a garbage bag over your backpack.
- ▨ Layer your clothes in three layers and have two sets.
- ▨ Never drink water from the creeks. Always use iodine to sterilize the water first. Follow directions closely.
- ▨ Powdered drinks can be carried in ziplock bags.
- ▨ Dried food is easy because it comes in pre-set portions.

Camping: RV

Toiletry Kit

☐ Add to Toiletry Kit - *see How To Pack Toiletry Kit — page 187-189*

☐ After-sun cream

☐ First-aid kit

☐ Insect repellent

☐ Sunscreen — highest number

☐ Zinc for nose

Clothes List

▨ This is a motor trip, there is plenty of room and each person can decide how much they need, so fill in the numbers that suit you.

☐ Bathrobe

☐ Jacket

☐ Hat

☐ Jeans

☐ Scarves

☐ Shoes

☐ Shorts

☐ Socks

☐ Tops

☐ Sleepwear

☐ Sunglasses

☐ Sweatshirt/sweater

☐ Swimsuit

☐ Thongs

☐ Underwear

EQUIPMENT

PART

3.⁵

CONTINUED

☐ 1 plastic bucket

☐ 1 laundry basket

☐ Portable grill

☐ Beach chairs — folding

☐ Extra blankets

☐ Broom/dustpan

☐ Can opener

☐ Corkscrew

☐ Cooking and grilling utensils

☐ Flashlights

☐ Insect repellent candles

☐ Lighting fluid

☐ Road maps

☐ Matches

☐ Paper or plastic plates/cups/bowls/glasses

☐ Paper napkins, paper towels, toilet paper

☐ Pots and pans

☐ Pillowcases

☐ Sleeping bags

☐ Swiss army knife

☐ Thermos

☐ Towels

TOOLS

- ☐ Ax
- ☐ Hammer
- ☐ Nails — assorted sizes
- ☐ Pliers
- ☐ Rope
- ☐ Screwdriver
- ☐ Shovel

PART
3.⁵

HINTS

- ▣ Forget the portable television and take along a supply of board games and books to read.

- ▣ The radio will keep you abreast of the news and the local weather.

- ▣ A long rope can be used to block off your camping spot when absent or as a line to dry clothes.

- ▣ Use the bucket to haul water, collect firewood or to wash out the laundry by hand.

- ▣ Use the laundry basket to haul wood, cart the laundry to the laundromat and bring it back again folded. Turn it upside down and use it as a tray.

- ▣ You can add other items — a coffee maker, tea pot — it depends on your personal needs for amenities.

Golf: Summer

PART
3.⁶

TOILETRY KIT

- [ ] Add to Toiletry Kit - *see How To Pack Toiletry Kit —
page 187-189*
- [ ] After-sun lotion
- [ ] Ben-gay or other cream for sore muscles
- [ ] Sunblock of highest number
- [ ] Zinc for nose

CLOTHES LIST

- [ ] 2 belts
- [ ] Blazer or jacket to dress up Bermuda shorts
and pants for dinner —M —W
- [ ] 4 outfits for dinner
- OR [ ] 4 skirts and tops
- [ ] 4 shorts —W
- [ ] 4 long pants - M
- [ ] 6 tops —M —W
- [ ] 1 golf glove
- [ ] Hat/visor that stays on
- [ ] Shoes
  - [ ] Golf shoes — no tennis shoes
  - [ ] Casual shoes for evening
- [ ] Sleepwear
- [ ] 6 pr golf socks

DAYS
7

WASH
1x**7**

- ☐ 4 pr socks for evening
- ☐ Sunglasses with dark lenses
- ☐ Swimsuit
- ☐ Swimsuit cover-up
- ☐ 2 ties —M
- ☐ 6 underwear

SPORTS EQUIPMENT

- ☐ Golf clubs and bag
- ☐ 2 boxes of golf balls for independent play

HINTS

◻ At most golf resorts, long pants are preferred for men. Women may wear culottes or Bermuda shorts.

◻ Polo shirts, not T-shirts, are preferred as tops. For women, a linen blend is excellent because it breathes. You will be working hard, so have a clean top for each day.

◻ Buy golf shoes, don't come with tennis shoes. If you are attending a clinic it is worthwhile. The pros take you more seriously and it gets you into the game mode.

◻ Watch a few games on television if you want to see how the pros play and what they are wearing.

Golf: Fall and Spring

PART
3.⁷

TOILETRY KIT

- [ ] Add to Toiletry Kit - *see How To Pack Toiletry Kit — page 187-189*
- [ ] After-sun lotion
- [ ] Ben-gay or other cream for sore muscles
- [ ] Sunscreen of a reasonable number
- [ ] Insect repellent

CLOTHES LIST

- [ ] 2 belts
- [ ] Blazer or jacket to dress up pants for dinner —M —W
- [ ] 4 outfits for dinner

OR
- [ ] 4 skirts and tops
- [ ] 4 long pants - M —W
- [ ] 6 shirts —M —W
- [ ] Hat/visor that stays on
- [ ] 1 golf glove
- [ ] Shoes
  - [ ] Golf shoes — no tennis shoes
  - [ ] Casual shoes for evening
- [ ] Sleepwear
- [ ] 6 pr golf socks
- [ ] 4 pr socks for evening

DAYS
7

WASH
1ˣ7

- ☐ Sunglasses
- ☐ 2 sweaters
- ☐ Swimsuit
- ☐ Swimsuit cover-up
- ☐ 2 ties —M
- ☐ 6 underwear

SPORTS EQUIPMENT

- ☐ Golf clubs and bag
- ☐ 2 boxes of golf balls for independent play

HINTS

▪ At most golf resorts, long pants are preferred for men. Women may wear culottes or Bermuda shorts, but it might be cool, so plan on long pants.

▪ Polo shirts, not T-shirts, are preferred as tops. For women, a linen blend is excellent because it breathes. It will be too cold for sleeveless in this season.

▪ Buy golf shoes, don't come with tennis shoes. If you are attending a clinic it is worthwhile. The pros take you more seriously and it gets you into the game mode.

▪ Watch a few games on television if you want to see how the pros play and what they are wearing.

Hiking

PART 3.⁸

TOILETRY KIT

- [ ] Add to Toiletry Kit - *see How To Pack Toiletry Kit — page 187-189*
- [ ] Adhesive tape and one pr of small plastic scissors with blunt ends
- [ ] Foot powders for soaking feet
- [ ] Foot liniment (homeopathic: arbor salve Tincture of Thuja Occidentalis in ointment base)
- [ ] Insect repellent
- [ ] Lip balm
- [ ] Medical kit designed for hikers
- [ ] Sunscreen
- [ ] Tincture of iodine pills to purify water

CLOTHES LIST

DAYS 7

WASH 2ˣ7

- [ ] Head covering — hat/scarf
- [ ] Hiking boots/trail boots
- [ ] 1 windbreaker — must block wind and rain
- [ ] 2 pr cotton pants — long or short depending on season
- [ ] 4 cotton T-shirts
- [ ] 3 pr padded cotton socks — long length with short pants and shorter length with long pants
- [ ] 3 underwear
- [ ] Scarf — tie around neck, can be used to mop brow

EQUIPMENT

☐ Backpack

☐ Binoculars

☐ Camera and film

☐ Compass

☐ Gloves — water repellent

☐ Guidebook

☐ Laundry bag

☐ Mirror

☐ 2 pr Sunglasses

☐ Swiss army knife

☐ Water bottle on belt or shoulder strap

☐ Walking staff with rubber tip for steep climb

☐ Whistle

PART
3.⁸

HINTS

▪ Don't take anything you haven't used before.

▪ When trying on boots take along a filled backpack, as more weight means wider feet. Be sure to break new boots in before your trip.

▪ Pants length: In the fall and spring wear long pants with elastic cuffs to keep out bugs and plant life. Wear short socks. If you wear Bermuda-length shorts, then wear long knee socks. Consider buying long pants that unzip to shorts.

▪ The color white is preferred for socks because blood from a wound is quickly seen.

▪ There is a difference between a *hike* and a *walk*. A hiker might not mind a walk, but a walker can not always hike. Be certain you know and understand what the plans include.

■ Don't put a Band-Aid on a blister: it rubs and makes it worse. Put a wide adhesive tape flat over the blister and it won't hurt anymore.

■ If going to a hot region, prepare at home by taking hot baths.

PART
3.8

CONTINUED

Sailing:
Yacht or Motor Yacht

All space is limited so pack accordingly. Clothes will be scrunched. Pack a duffle bag and store it under your mattress. Hang space is limited to non-existent.

Toiletry Kit

Toiletry Kit — *see How to Pack Toiletry Kit —* *page 187-189*

Amend toiletry bag to take only travel/sample size as head (wc) and shower — if there is one — are compact.

Motion-sickness medication

Clothes List

1 pr jeans or long pants

Rain wear with sou'wester hat — yellow

OR Rain coat/hat — yellow

2 pr shorts

4 pr socks

2 pr shoes — tie-on, rubber-soled shoes with tread i.e. canvas/deck/running/tennis shoes

Sleepwear

1 sweatshirt

1 sweatpants

1 pullover sweater

- [ ] Swimsuit
- [ ] 3 tank tops — any season — use as layers in winter
- [ ] 2 long-sleeved T-shirts
- [ ] 2 short-sleeved T-shirts
- [ ] Underwear
- [ ] Watchman's cap — like the ones long-shoremen wear
- [ ] Windbreaker — lightweight, waterproof, bright-colored

PART
3.⁹
CONTINUED

Hints

- No metal zippers or pocket grommets. Most yachts have lots of wood decks, even railings that can scratch easily. Check your clothes carefully. Scratched wood can ruin a friendship.

- Don't wear the color navy blue - it is hard to see if you are washed overboard.

- Take sleepwear even if you are not used to wearing it. It's necessary in such a small space. In winter make it flannel.

- Think of clothes that fold since hang space is limited, and think of clothes you can put on in layers.

- Wear shoes that tie on or are fitting so they don't fall off. Don't take thongs unless they are for on land, and only in the summer. No heels, only rubber-soled flats.

- In fall and spring add 1 pr long cotton pants and take only 1 pr of shorts. Bring boots or galoshes and 1 pr thick socks for inside boots.

- Hostess gift: foods that can be eaten on the trip — if packaged, preferably not glass, as in a bottle of wine. If your host has a power boat don't bring a gift with a sail on it and vice versa. Don't bring cute knickknacks. Odd shaped things are difficult to store in small square storage places.

☐ If you have been invited to sail or cruise on a private yacht ask: is it a powerboat (more room) or a sailboat (less room).

Skiing Vacation: Anywhere U.S.

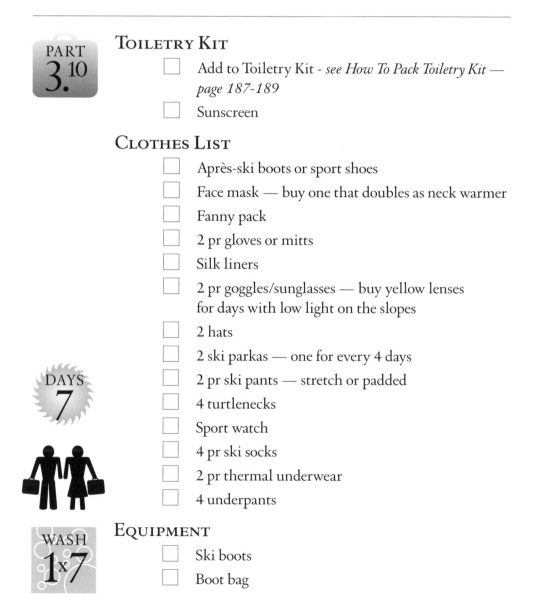

PART 3.10

TOILETRY KIT

- [ ] Add to Toiletry Kit - *see How To Pack Toiletry Kit — page 187-189*
- [ ] Sunscreen

CLOTHES LIST

- [ ] Après-ski boots or sport shoes
- [ ] Face mask — buy one that doubles as neck warmer
- [ ] Fanny pack
- [ ] 2 pr gloves or mitts
- [ ] Silk liners
- [ ] 2 pr goggles/sunglasses — buy yellow lenses for days with low light on the slopes
- [ ] 2 hats
- [ ] 2 ski parkas — one for every 4 days
- [ ] 2 pr ski pants — stretch or padded
- [ ] 4 turtlenecks
- [ ] Sport watch
- [ ] 4 pr ski socks
- [ ] 2 pr thermal underwear
- [ ] 4 underpants

DAYS 7

EQUIPMENT

- [ ] Ski boots
- [ ] Boot bag

WASH 1x7

- [ ] Binding covers
- [ ] Poles
- [ ] Skis
- [ ] Ski bag for airline travel. If skis are new, first wrap in bubble wrap.

OPTIONAL

- [ ] Boot carrier to get to slopes
- [ ] Boot/glove dryer
- [ ] Cat tracks
- [ ] Ski pass holder for arm or jacket zipper
- [ ] Ski lock
- [ ] Tuning supplies — one set for the family

HINT

- Most airlines consider ski bag and boot bag as one piece of luggage. If not, they charge for excess baggage.

CLOTHES LIST FOR APRÈS SKI

- [ ] 2 belts
- [ ] 1 blazer jacket
- [ ] Casual outerwear jacket
- [ ] Hat
- [ ] Gloves
- [ ] 4 pantyhose and/or socks
- [ ] Shoes
  - [ ] dress shoes or comfortable shoes
  - [ ] slippers/thongs/health sandals optional
  - [ ] sport - tennis/canvas
- [ ] 3 shirts or tops
- [ ] 3 skirts

OR ☐ 3 pr of slacks —M —W

OR ☐ 3 pr of slacks and 1 skirt and 2 leggings

OR ☐ Jeans — in the U.S.

☐ 3 sweaters

☐ Swimsuit — many resorts have a pool

☐ 1 sleepwear — flannel

☐ 1 tie — for the splurge dinner —M

☐ 4 underwear

☐ Scarf for jacket

PART

3.10

CONTINUED

HINTS

Hotels offer laundry service if you take your cleaning to the front desk at breakfast time.

Condos and Apartments all have washing machines and dryers. Take a bank roll of quarters.

What you wear after skiing is determined by where you are staying and what you plan to do after skiing. Casual dress is fine if you are in a condo. If you are staying at a hotel, dressing for dinner is the norm but can be jeans with a nice sweater.

Have your equipment checked before you go.

If you are new to the sport, buy your ski boots at your destination. Wherever you are is a long way from your local ski shop if they are not comfortable.

Skiing Europe: Winter

TOILETRY KIT

☐ Add to Toiletry Kit - *see How To Pack Toiletry Kit — page 187-189*

☐ Sunscreen

CLOTHES LIST

☐ Après-ski boots

☐ Face mask — buy one that doubles as neck warmer

☐ Fanny pack

☐ 2 pr gloves or mitts

☐ Silk liners

☐ 2 pr goggles/sunglasses - buy yellow lenses for days with low light on the slopes

☐ 2 hats

☐ 2 ski parkas — 1 for every 4 days — with a hood for mid-winter

☐ 2 pr ski pants — stretch or padded but padded is warmer. Watch out for slick fabrics. You'll slide off the piste or into the path of a skier if you fall

☐ 6 turtlenecks

☐ Sport watch

☐ 6 pr ski socks

☐ 2 pr thermal underwear

☐ 6 underpants

EQUIPMENT

- ☐ Ski boots
- ☐ Boot bag
- ☐ Binding covers
- ☐ Poles
- ☐ Skis
- ☐ Ski bag for airline travel. If skis are new, wrap first in bubble wrap

PART
3.¹¹

CONTINUED

OPTIONAL

- ☐ Boot carrier to get to slopes
- ☐ Boot/glove dryer
- ☐ Cat tracks
- ☐ Special holder for your ski ticket. One model fits on your upper arm and you slip the ski pass in. Another type is a cord hooked to your parka zipper that pulls and retracts to run the pass through the meter at the bottom of the lift.
- ☐ Ski lock
- ☐ Tuning supplies — one set for family

ASK

- ▨ Most airlines consider ski bag and boot bag as one piece of luggage. Otherwise they'll charge for excess baggage.

CLOTHES LIST - APRÈS SKI

- ☐ 2 belts
- ☐ 1 blazer jacket
- ☐ Casual outerwear jacket — see note on fur coat
- ☐ Gloves
- ☐ Hat
- ☐ 6 pantyhose and/or socks

☐ Shoes
  ☐ dress shoes or comfortable shoes
  ☐ slippers/thongs/health sandals optional
  ☐ sport — not for dinner
☐ 4 shirts or tops —M —W
☐ 4 skirts
OR ☐ 4 pr of slacks —M —W
OR ☐ 4 pr of slacks and 2 skirts and 2 leggings —W
☐ 4 sweaters
☐ Swimsuit — many resorts have a pool
☐ Sleepwear
☐ 4 ties —M
☐ 6 underwear
☐ Scarf for coat

PART
3.11

HINTS

▢ Hotels offer next afternoon laundry service. Take any clothes for cleaning to the front desk at breakfast time.

▢ If you want to pack less, plan to wash socks and underwear in the sinks. You can hang them to dry in the bathroom, or over the radiator.

▢ What you wear après ski depends on your lodging. If you are staying in a condo, a casual style of clothes is fine. If you are booked in a hotel, dressing up for dinner is expected. Dressing up may be whatever your style is, but jeans, unless you are younger, will be out of place.

▢ Fur coats for men and women are accepted as part of the scene.

▢ Body suit for outer ski wear - remember it all has to come off at the wc.

Have your equipment checked before you go.

Buy your new boots at your skiing destination if you are new to this. Europe is a long way from your local ski shop.

PART
3.11

CONTINUED

Skiing Europe: Spring

TOILETRY KIT

- [ ] Add to Toiletry Kit - *see How To Pack Toiletry Kit — page 187-189*
- [ ] Sunscreen
- [ ] Zinc for nose and lips

CLOTHES LIST

- [ ] Après-ski boots
- [ ] Fanny pack
- [ ] 2 pr gaiters to go over boots
- [ ] 2 pr gloves or mitts
- [ ] 2 pr sunglasses — sun will be stronger longer, so take darker lenses as well
- [ ] 2 headbands
- [ ] 1 ski parka with zip-out sleeves
- [ ] 1 wind jacket

- [ ] 2 pr ski pants —watch out for slick fabrics. You'll slide off the piste or into the path of a skier if you fall

- OR [ ] 2 pr windbreaker pants
- OR [ ] 2 pr side-zip pants with jeans or just long underwear underneath

- [ ] 6 turtlenecks or long-sleeved shirts.
- [ ] Ski sweater — a lightweight one that dispels moisture

- ☐ Sport watch
- ☐ 6 pr ski socks
- ☐ 2 pr thermal underwear
- ☐ 6 underpants

EQUIPMENT

- ☐ Ski boots
- ☐ Boot bag
- ☐ Binding covers
- ☐ Poles
- ☐ Skis
- ☐ Ski bag for airline travel. If skis are new, first wrap them in bubble wrap

PART
3.¹²
CONTINUED

OPTIONAL

- ☐ Boot carrier to get to slopes
- ☐ Boot/glove dryer
- ☐ Cat tracks
- ☐ Special holder for your ski ticket — one model fits on your upper arm and you slip the ski pass in. Another type is a cord hooked to your parka zipper that pulls and retracts to run the pass through the meter at the bottom of the lift.
- ☐ Ski lock
- ☐ Tuning supplies — one set for the family

CLOTHES LIST - APRÈS SKI

- ☐ 2 belts
- ☐ 1 blazer jacket
- ☐ Casual outerwear jacket
- ☐ 6 pantyhose and/or socks
- ☐ Shoes
  - ☐ dress shoes or comfortable shoes

☐ slippers/thongs/health sandals optional

☐ sport — not for dinner

☐ 4 shirts or tops —M —W

☐ 4 skirts

Or ☐ 4 pr of slacks —M —W

Or ☐ 4 pr of slacks and 2 skirts and 2 leggings —W

☐ 4 sweaters

☐ Swimsuit - many resorts have a pool

☐ Sleepwear/T-shirt

☐ 4 ties —M

☐ 6 underwear

PART
3.¹²

HINTS

Hotels offer next-afternoon laundry service if you take your clothes to the front desk at breakfast time.

If you want to pack less, plan to wash socks and underwear in sink. You can hang them to dry in the bathroom, or over the radiator.

What you wear après ski depends on your lodging. If you are staying in a condo, a casual style of clothes is fine. If you are booked in a hotel, dressing up for dinner is expected. Dressing up may be whatever your style is, but jeans, unless you are younger, will be out of place.

Skiing: Cross Country

PART
3.¹³

Moisture is your major concern. When purchasing clothes, ask about moisture retention. Too much cotton inhibits thermal properties. Baggy is better.

TOILETRY KIT

- [ ] Add to Toiletry Kit - *see How To Pack Toiletry Kit — page 187-189*
- [ ] Moleskin kit for blisters
- [ ] Lip balm
- [ ] Sunscreen

CLOTHES LIST

- [ ] Fanny pack
- [ ] 2 hats
- [ ] 2 pr knee-high gaiters for deep snow
- [ ] 2 neck gaiters
- [ ] Sunglasses
- [ ] 3 thermal underwear
- [ ] 2 sets of layered outerwear consisting of pants and jacket
- [ ] 4 turtlenecks

DAYS
7

EQUIPMENT

- [ ] Boot bag
- [ ] Boots
- [ ] Poles

WASH
2x7

☐ Skis

☐ Ski bag

CLOTHES LIST FOR APRÈS-SKI

☐ 2 belts

☐ Casual outerwear jacket

☐ Hat

☐ Gloves

☐ 4 pantyhose and/or socks

☐ Shoes

     ☐ slippers/thongs/health sandals optional

     ☐ sport

☐ 3 shirts or tops

☐ 3 pr slacks and 1 skirt and 2 leggings —M —W

Or ☐ Jeans only in the U.S. —M —W

☐ 3 sweaters

☐ Swimsuit — many resorts have a pool

☐ Sleepwear

☐ 1 tie — for the splurge restaurant —M

☐ 4 underwear

☐ Scarf for jacket

PART
3.13

Tennis Clinic or Resort

Part 3.14

Toiletry Kit

- [ ] Add to Toiletry Kit - *see How To Pack Toiletry Kit — page 187-189*
- [ ] After-sun lotion
- [ ] Bengay or other cream for sore muscles
- [ ] Insecticide/insect repellent
- [ ] Sunscreen — highest number
- [ ] Zinc for nose

Clothes List

- [ ] 2 belts
- [ ] Blazer or jacket to dress up Bermuda shorts and pants for dinner —M —W
- [ ] 4 dresses for dinner
- OR [ ] 4 skirts and tops
- [ ] 6 shorts —M —W
- [ ] 6 tops —M —W
- [ ] 4 long pants —M
- [ ] Sleepwear
- [ ] Shoes
  - [ ] dress shoes for evening
  - [ ] sandals
  - [ ] 2 pr tennis shoes
- [ ] Sun visor or hat

Days 7

Wash 1x7

☐ Sunglasses with dark lenses
☐ Swimsuit
☐ Swimsuit cover up
☐ 4 ties —M
☐ 6 pr tennis socks
☐ 5 pr socks for evening wear
☐ 6 underwear

SPORTS EQUIPMENT

☐ Tennis racket plus spare if you have it
☐ Tennis racket cover
☐ Grip tape
☐ Tennis bag for travelling

HINTS

▪ Ask in advance if the resort requires all-white tennis clothes before you buy outfits in colors.

▪ To this destination it is acceptable to wear leisure suits on the plane. If young, sweats are fine as it looks right for tennis resorts. Choose shoes accordingly.

▪ All-cotton sleepwear. All-cotton underwear. Plan to wash underwear to have enough for the week.

▪ Shoes should be broken in to prevent blisters. Remember more heat means more sweat and more rubbing. A second pair of tennis shoes is a good idea.

▪ Swimming and other sports will be available.

▪ Dress requirements for dinner will vary with the resort.

PART 4

What to Pack

for "Dream Weekends"

WITH TRAVEL TIME OF A 3-DAY WEEKEND

Big City: In an Apartment

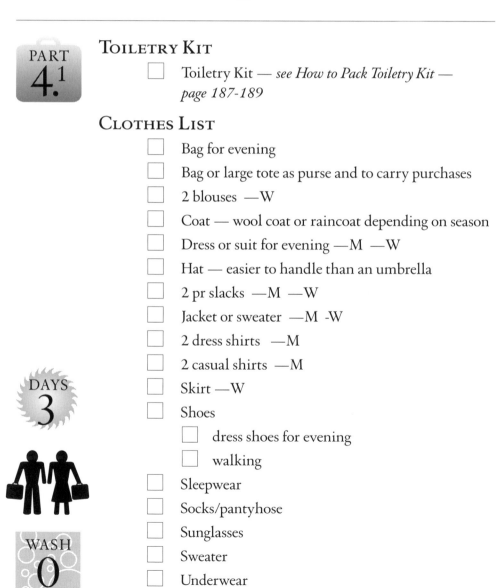

PART 4.[1]

TOILETRY KIT

☐ Toiletry Kit — *see How to Pack Toiletry Kit — page 187-189*

CLOTHES LIST

☐ Bag for evening

☐ Bag or large tote as purse and to carry purchases

☐ 2 blouses —W

☐ Coat — wool coat or raincoat depending on season

☐ Dress or suit for evening —M —W

☐ Hat — easier to handle than an umbrella

☐ 2 pr slacks —M —W

☐ Jacket or sweater —M -W

☐ 2 dress shirts —M

☐ 2 casual shirts —M

☐ Skirt —W

☐ Shoes

    ☐ dress shoes for evening

    ☐ walking

☐ Sleepwear

☐ Socks/pantyhose

☐ Sunglasses

☐ Sweater

☐ Underwear

DAYS 3

WASH 0

EQUIPMENT

- ☐ Camera and film

- ☐ Take your hair dryer because the absent apartment owner has likely taken the one they have.

- ☐ Take a large bag with shoulder straps to carry purchases. Anything carried by hand might be forgotten.

- ☐ Opera glasses — if you don't know the theatre seating, you might be farther away than you think.

- ☐ Quarters for washer and dryer if you need to use them.

HINTS

- ☐ *Do not*: Do not wear shorts. Do not wear open shoes. Your feet get dirty and this type of shoe is not comfortable for walking any distance. Do not wear jeans when slacks are better.

- ☐ Do not wear a red jacket to the Kennedy Center in Washington D.C. You will look like one of the ushers.

- ☐ If you are having breakfast at the apartment, buy basic groceries for breakfast: coffee, tea, milk, small sugar, bread, butter, fruit, jam, crackers, cheese — whatever suits you.

- ☐ It is disheartening to come back to one's apartment on Monday morning and find all the basics used up. It is wonderful to come back and find little extras.

- ☐ Put away all food. Cockroaches thrive in big cities.

- ☐ Replenish the toilet paper. Return everything to where you found it. Wash all dishes.

☐ Take your own toiletries. Don't even think of using the owners supply.

☐ Wash out bathtub and sink and throw dirty towels in the hamper if the owner is returning next day, if not returning immediately, wash towels or leave hanging. Wet towels mildew when left in hamper.

☐ If you break something, replace it or leave note and money. Don't ignore it.

☐ If apartment is on loan to you, buy a present in the city where you are. You can buy according to the style and taste of the owner. If you have rented, leave a tip for the cleaning service.

Big City:
In a Hotel

TOILETRY KIT

☐ Toiletry Kit — *see How to Pack Toiletry Kit* —
page 187-189

▨ Hotels supply bubble bath, lotions, sewing kit,
shampoo, shower caps and soaps. Adjust your
cosmetics.

CLOTHES LIST

☐ Bag for evening

☐ Bag or large tote as purse and to carry purchases

☐ 3 blouses —W

☐ Coat — wool coat or raincoat depending on season

☐ Dress or suit for evening —M —W

☐ Hat — easier to handle than umbrella

☐ 2 dress shirts —M

☐ 2 casual shirts —M

☐ 2 pr slacks —M —W

☐ Jacket or sweater

☐ Jewelry

☐ Skirt

☐ Shoes

  ☐ dress shoes for evening

  ☐ walking

☐ Sleepwear

PART
4.²

DAYS
3

WASH
0

- ☐ Socks/pantyhose
- ☐ Sunglasses
- ☐ Sweater
- ☐ Underwear

EQUIPMENT

- ☐ Camera and film

HINTS

PART
4.²
CONTINUED

- ☐ Hair dryer — the more expensive the hotel, the better chance that there is one hanging on the bathroom wall.

- ☐ Jewelry - thefts occur. It is best to wear what you need. Carry extras with you in the bottom of your purse or put them in the hotel safe.

- ☐ Take a large bag with shoulder straps to carry purchases. Anything carried by hand might be forgotten.

- ☐ Opera glasses — if you don't know the theatre seating arrangement, you might be farther away than you think.

- ☐ *Do not*. Do not wear shorts. Do not wear open shoes. Your feet get dirty and these shoes are not comfortable over distance. Do not wear jeans when slacks are better.

- ☐ Do not wear a red jacket to the Kennedy Center in Washington D.C. You will look like one of the ushers.

London Weekend

TOILETRY KIT

☐ Toiletry Kit — *see How to Pack Toiletry Kit* — *page 187-189*

CLOTHES LIST

☐ Blazer Jacket —M —W

☐ Coat — raincoat with liner

☐ 1 dressy top —W

☐ Gloves

☐ Hat or umbrella

☐ Warm robe

☐ Muffler or scarf

☐ 3 blouses/shirts —M —W

☐ Shoes

    ☐ casual walking - no sport shoes!

    ☐ dress walking

☐ 2 slacks —M

☐ 2 skirts or 2 slacks —W one should match dressy top

☐ 4 pr warm socks

☐ 3 sweaters

☐ Sleepwear

☐ Slippers — every season but summer

☐ 3 ties

DAYS 4

WASH 0

☐ Long underwear — every season but summer

☐ Warm underwear - fall, winter, spring

CONTINUED

London and the Theatre

PART
4.⁴

- [ ] American - British dictionary
- [ ] Chocolates for intermission
- [ ] Coat — one to wad up on lap to avoid post-theatre cloak room crush
- [ ] Kleenex for Loo (w.c.) use — gospel truth — good to have if the play is a tear-jerker
- [ ] Money for program - it is not free
- [ ] Money for refreshment at intermission - if you don't believe it about the chocolates
- [ ] Opera glasses
- [ ] Reading glasses for program.
- [ ] Small scrapbook — put souvenir stubs in it now
- [ ] Text of Play
- [ ] Tickets
- [ ] Underground map & ticket - cabs are mobbed post performance

HINT

Do not take chewing gum or a watch that beeps, calls or makes noise. If it can go off, it will.

Cabin in the Woods: Weekend

PART

4.⁵

TOILETRY KIT

☐ Toiletry Kit — *see How to Pack Toiletry Kit — page 187-189*

CLOTHES LIST

☐ Boots — calf-high Maine boots or lace-up

☐ 2 pr jeans

☐ Mittens — heavy

☐ Parka/jacket — hooded, with fleece lining, no flashy colors, sometimes called a 4-in-1 jacket

☐ Scarf — woolen

☐ Sleepwear — flannel

☐ Slippers — floors are cold.

☐ 1 pr casual shoes for indoors — your choice

☐ 3 pr cotton socks

☐ 2 pr woolen socks for boots

☐ Heavy wool sweater (knit by your aunt)

☐ Wool cardigan sweater — instead of blazer

☐ 3 cotton turtleneck shirts

☐ 3 long-sleeved shirts (plaid of course)

☐ Underwear

DAYS

3

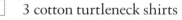

WASH

0

HINTS

☐ As a guest you should know there will be wood to haul, dishes to wash, chores you might not be used to in your other life. *Offer to help.*

☐ Hostess gift: Basket gifts, bottled gifts, food items.

PART
4.⁵

Cape Cod Weekend: Summer

TOILETRY KIT

☐ Toiletry Kit — *see How to Pack Toiletry Kit* —
page 187-189

CLOTHES LIST

☐ Anorak/car coat or cotton parka, but not
the flashy kind worn skiing

☐ 2 belts

☐ Blazer jacket for dinner. —M

☐ Canvas tote bag for shopping, the shore
or to wherever

☐ Hats: straw for the shore; cotton bush hat for
in-town, a visor for tennis

☐ Sunglasses

☐ Jewelry in gold, but not too much

☐ 1 chambray long-sleeved shirt or
jeans shirt —M —W

☐ 2 cotton duck pants or jeans

☐ 2 blouses —W

☐ 2 polo shirts in solid colors

☐ 2 solid-color oxford shirts

☐ 2 shorts — madras

OR ☐ 2 shorts — solid color or white

DAYS
3

WASH
0

- ☐ Shoes
  - ☐ canvas deck/espadrilles
  - ☐ tennis
  - ☐ leather loafers
  - ☐ thongs — double as slippers
- ☐ 2 skirts or 2 long pants - W
- ☐ 3 pr socks for day
- ☐ 2 pr socks for evening
- ☐ Swimsuit — boxer style —M
- ☐ Swimsuit cover-up
- ☐ Sweater — Irish fisherman or hooded sweatshirt
- ☐ 2 ties

SPORTS

- ☐ Possibly all-white clothes for tennis.
- ☐ Ask what sports will be played and plan accordingly.

HINTS

- ▨ *Do Pack*: anything that is "understated chic," anything that says "old money," anything that says "used to have old money but gave it all to a good cause." Signet ring & family crest.

- ▨ Take a hostess gift of bottled oils or vinegars or special condiments or fancy teas.

- ▨ *Do not pack*: flashy colors, flashy clothes, or anything that is too "citified." Jeans and checkered anything are for the ranch out west. Skimpy European bathing suits are déclassé.

College Family Weekend: Men

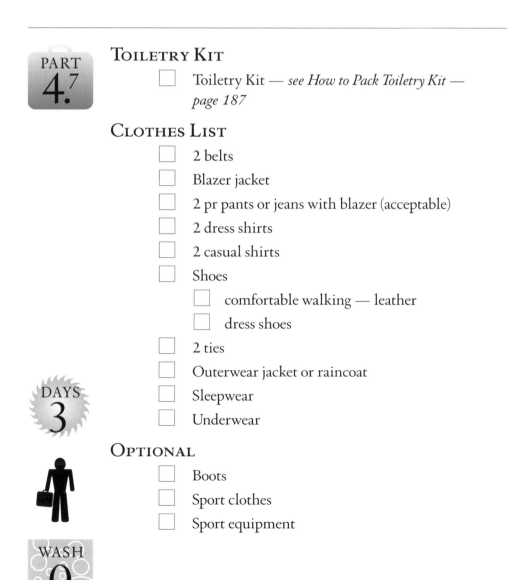

PART

4.⁷

Toiletry Kit

☐ Toiletry Kit — *see How to Pack Toiletry Kit —
page 187*

Clothes List

☐ 2 belts

☐ Blazer jacket

☐ 2 pr pants or jeans with blazer (acceptable)

☐ 2 dress shirts

☐ 2 casual shirts

☐ Shoes

    ☐ comfortable walking — leather

    ☐ dress shoes

☐ 2 ties

☐ Outerwear jacket or raincoat

☐ Sleepwear

☐ Underwear

DAYS

3

Optional

☐ Boots

☐ Sport clothes

☐ Sport equipment

WASH

0

HINT

If you cannot change between the "address" and the "picnic," wear slacks and jacket. You can sit on the grass, take off the jacket and put the tie in your pocket.

College Family Weekend: Women

PART 4.8

TOILETRY KIT

- [ ] Toiletry Kit — *see How to Pack Toiletry Kit — page 189*

CLOTHES LIST

- [ ] Blazer jacket
- [ ] Coat — dressy with scarf for looks and/or warmth but good over slacks
- [ ] 2 dresses/or suit to wear to address by President. Also can wear to "reception"
- [ ] Gloves
- [ ] Jewelry
- [ ] Shoes
  - [ ] comfortable walking shoes
  - [ ] dress shoes
- [ ] 1 shorts and top — might be warm fall day for picnic
- [ ] 2 skirts
- [ ] 1 slacks — wool
- [ ] 1 cotton sweater — wool for colder weather
- [ ] 1 cardigan sweater
- [ ] 4 tops
- [ ] Sleepwear
- [ ] Underwear

DAYS 3

WASH 0

HINTS

 For colder weather add a sweater and socks and heavy shoes.

 Plan early.

 Book a hotel close to campus, if at all possible, within walking distance. Some schools offer a dorm room. If weather changes during the day, you can change your outfit.

Farm Weekend

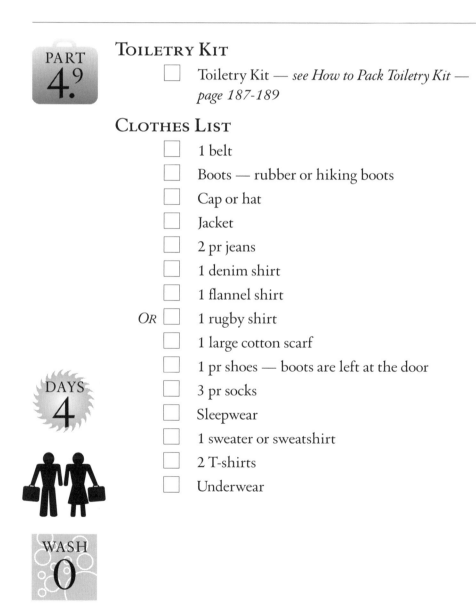

PART 4.⁹

TOILETRY KIT

- [ ] Toiletry Kit — *see How to Pack Toiletry Kit — page 187-189*

CLOTHES LIST

- [ ] 1 belt
- [ ] Boots — rubber or hiking boots
- [ ] Cap or hat
- [ ] Jacket
- [ ] 2 pr jeans
- [ ] 1 denim shirt
- [ ] 1 flannel shirt
- *OR* [ ] 1 rugby shirt
- [ ] 1 large cotton scarf
- [ ] 1 pr shoes — boots are left at the door
- [ ] 3 pr socks
- [ ] Sleepwear
- [ ] 1 sweater or sweatshirt
- [ ] 2 T-shirts
- [ ] Underwear

DAYS **4**

WASH **0**

HINTS

- In summer, add two pairs of shorts, but still take the rubber boots.

- If this is a working farm, you might be expected to help, so pack clothes that can rise to the occasion.

- Take a plastic bag to put your muddy, dirty clothes in for the trip home.

PART
4.9

Homeward Bound Weekend

PART
4.¹⁰

TOILETRY KIT

☐ Toiletry Kit — *see How to Pack Toiletry Kit — page 187-189* (don't need anything the folks probably have it all ready for you)

CLOTHES LIST

☐ Casual clothes for two days

☐ Casual shoes

☐ One decent outfit for dinner home one night. Let your parents know you still have "decent clothes" with proper shoes- no sneakers

☐ Pajamas and robe for breakfast

HINTS

☐ Thank-you present

☐ Pictures. Those at home want to see who it is you talk or write about.

DAYS
3

STUDENTS

◼ Pack your dirty wash. If you don't know how much room it takes packed, it will get very rumpled after it is clean. This is your chance to have Mom take the pink tint out of the wash assortment that came about from the first on-your-own-load.

All your dirty wash

"Inn" the Country: Weekend

TOILETRY KIT

- [ ] Toiletry Kit — *see How to Pack Toiletry Kit — page 187-189*

CLOTHES LIST

- [ ] Blazer jacket —M —W
- [ ] 1 dressy top —W
- [ ] 3 blouses/tops —W
- [ ] 2 dress shirts —M
- [ ] Shoes
  - [ ] casual walking
  - [ ] dress for evening
  - [ ] sport shoes for bicycling
- [ ] 4 slacks —M
- [ ] 2 skirts and 2 slacks — one should match dressy top —W
- [ ] 4 pr socks
- [ ] 2 sweaters
- [ ] Sleepwear
- [ ] 3 ties —M
- [ ] Underwear

HINTS

At the time you make your reservations find out how dressed up you need to be for the dining room.

PART
4.11
CONTINUED

- Dining is usually the main event of such a weekend. Ask for particulars at time of booking.

- During the day the activities include walking, bicycling and local shopping.

- If this is a three-day - two-night package, plan to dress for two evening meals. Jacket and tie might be required for men. Dressy pants are fine for women in place of skirts and dresses.

- Most inns do not have swimming pools, so only if going to a lake or the ocean do you need to take a swimming suit.

Long Island Weekend: Summer

Toiletry Kit

☐ Toiletry Kit — *see How to Pack Toiletry Kit — page 187-189*

Clothes List

☐ 3 belts

☐ Blazer jacket for dinner —M

☐ Canvas tote bag to carry shopping, to shore, to wherever

☐ Dress or fancy jump suit for evening —W

☐ Hats: straw for the water, cotton bush hat for in-town, visor for tennis

☐ 2 pr sunglasses

☐ Jewelry in gold, never can have too much

☐ 1 chambray long-sleeved shirt —M —W

☐ 2 pr cotton duck pants — sometimes called chinos

Or ☐ 1 dressy warm-up/leisure-wear suit

☐ 2 cotton T-shirts in plain white

☐ 4 polo shirts in solid colors

☐ 2 solid color oxford shirts

☐ 2 shorts — solid color

☐ 2 shorts — white

☐ Shoes

☐ canvas deck/espadrilles

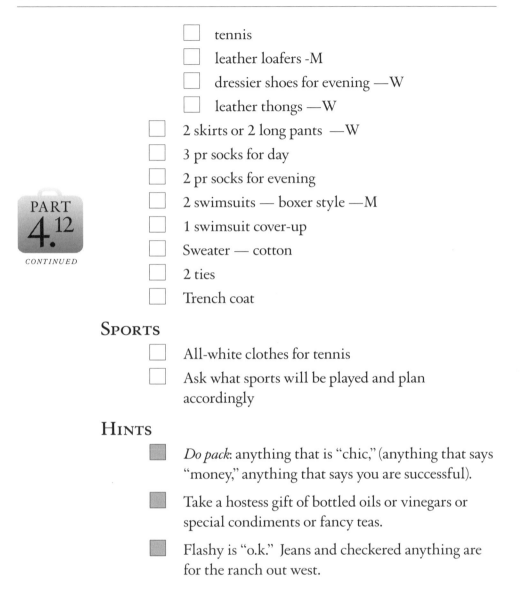

- [ ] tennis
- [ ] leather loafers -M
- [ ] dressier shoes for evening —W
- [ ] leather thongs —W
- [ ] 2 skirts or 2 long pants —W
- [ ] 3 pr socks for day
- [ ] 2 pr socks for evening
- [ ] 2 swimsuits — boxer style —M
- [ ] 1 swimsuit cover-up
- [ ] Sweater — cotton
- [ ] 2 ties
- [ ] Trench coat

PART
4.12
CONTINUED

Sports

- [ ] All-white clothes for tennis
- [ ] Ask what sports will be played and plan accordingly

Hints

- *Do pack:* anything that is "chic," (anything that says "money," anything that says you are successful).

- Take a hostess gift of bottled oils or vinegars or special condiments or fancy teas.

- Flashy is "o.k." Jeans and checkered anything are for the ranch out west.

New England Weekend: Winter

TOILETRY KIT

- [ ] Toiletry Kit — *see How to Pack Toiletry Kit — page 187-189*

CLOTHES LIST

- [ ] 1 belt
- [ ] Boots — Maine boots or après-ski boots
- [ ] Car coat/parka /4-in-1 jacket
- [ ] Gloves — deerskin or shearling
- [ ] Hat: knitted cap, beret, your choice, but it must stay on
- [ ] Muffler/scarf
- [ ] 2 pr corduroy trousers
- [ ] 1 Shoes — suede bucks or classic loafer
- [ ] 1 denim shirt
- [ ] 1 flannel shirt
- [ ] 1 corduroy shirt

OR
- [ ] 1 long-sleeved rugby shirt but in subdued hues

OR
- [ ] 1 long-sleeved polo shirt with turtleneck underneath

- [ ] 3 T-shirts or turtlenecks
- [ ] 4 pr socks
- [ ] Slippers — floors can be cold
- [ ] Sleepwear — flannel

- [ ] Sweater — navy crew
- [ ] Underwear

SPORTS

- [ ] Sweatshirt and sweatpants. Ask what activities are planned in case you need more T-shirts.

HINT

- [ ] It might be colder than expected.

PART

4.13

CONTINUED

Sailing Yacht or Cabin Cruiser: Weekend

All space is limited so pack accordingly. Clothes will scrunched. Pack a duffle bag and store it under your mattress. Hang space is limited.

PART
4.14

TOILETRY KIT

☐ Toiletry Kit — *see How to Pack Toiletry Kit — page 187-189*

☐ Amend toiletry bag to take only travel/sample size, as head (wc) and shower — if there is one — are compact.

☐ Motion-sickness medication

CLOTHES LIST

☐ Boots/galoshes — except in summer

☐ 1 pr jeans or long pants — summer

☐ Rain wear, yellow in color with sou'wester hat

OR ☐ Rain coat and hat, yellow in color

☐ 2 pr shorts

☐ 4 pr socks

☐ 1 pr thick socks for inside boots —except in summer

☐ 2 pr shoes — tie-on, rubber-soled shoes with tread i.e. canvas/deck/running/tennis shoes

☐ Sleepwear

☐ 1 sweatshirt

DAYS
3

WASH
0

- [ ] 1 sweatpants
- [ ] 1 pullover sweater
- [ ] Swimsuit
- [ ] 3 tank tops — summer or winter — use as layers in winter
- [ ] 2 long-sleeved T-shirts
- [ ] 2 short-sleeved T-shirts
- [ ] Underwear
- [ ] Watchman's cap — like the ones longshoremen wear
- [ ] Windbreaker — lightweight, waterproof, bright-colored

PART

4.¹⁴

CONTINUED

HINTS

- No metal zippers or pocket grommets. Most yachts have lots of wood decks, even railings, and they scratch easily. Check your clothes carefully.

- Don't wear the color navy blue — it is hard to see if you fall overboard.

- In such a small space take sleepwear even if you are not used to wearing it. Make it flannel in cooler seasons.

- Pack clothes that fold since hang space is limited. Pack clothes you can wear in layers.

- Wear shoes that tie on or are snug fitting so they don't fall off. Don't take thongs unless it's summer and only for going ashore. No heels, only flats with rubber soles.

- If you have been invited to sail or cruise on a private yacht ask if its a powerboat (more room) or a sailboat (less room).

☐ Hostess gift: packaged foods to be eaten on trip. No glass, so no bottle of wine. No cute knickknacks. Odd- shaped things are difficult to store in small square storage places.

☐ If your host has a powerboat, don't bring a gift with a sail on it and vice versa.

PART 5

What to Pack

for Travel with Children & Babies

Airplanes and Babies

PART 5.1

EQUIPMENT

- [ ] Soft-sided bag. Pack everything for baby in a soft-sided bag. It fits under the seat and as items are used, the bag takes up less space.
- [ ] Additional top for warmth or climate control
- [ ] Baby blanket
- [ ] Bottle - plastic filled with juice/water/milk/formula
- [ ] Disposable diapers plus diaper liner for easier changing. One diaper change per flight hour
- [ ] Pacifier — helps relieve ear pressure
- [ ] Toys — soft materials/cloth baby books
- [ ] Washcloth in plastic bag or disposable wipes
- [ ] Stroller

HINTS

- Dress baby in one-piece outfit that opens at the legs. Two pieces separate and are drafty. Cold babies cry. Sweats material is comfortable and non-constricting. Pack a second outfit in soft-sided bag for clean-up before arrival.

- Take outfits that are interchangeable and use clothes in layers for climate control. When it is colder, add layers, when it warms up, remove them.

▫ Do not pack dry food that makes crumbs or cereals that litter seating area.

▫ Reserve bulkhead seat with bed if available on airline.

▫ Pack a baby carrier for use anywhere. There will be times when a stroller is not convenient, but a carrier is. One such place is the aisle of an airplane.

Airplanes and Children

PART
5.²

CLOTHES FOR CHILDREN

☐ Comfortable clothes and shoes. Layered outfits allow adjustment to temperature changes. If it is a long flight, less clothes for waking period, more clothes for sleeping.

ADULT CLOTHES

☐ Comfortable, easy, non-binding. Avoid colors that show spots and spills. This may be a business trip, but unless the client is meeting you at the gate, skip the business suit.

☐ Limit adult hand luggage. It gets in the way coming, going and sitting.

CHILD CARRY-ON

☐ Back pack with toys especially for cramped space; new books, pop up books, soft books. If foreign land-bound, buy language play-and-learn books

☐ Bottle of water — plastic

☐ Card games

☐ Food snack — supplements airline food

☐ Hand-held games

☐ Kleenex — mini pack

☐ Nose spray — for pressure relief. Nose spray relieves the pressure in the ears better than sucking

on candy. Spray in child's nose before take-off
and landing.

☐ Peel-and-stick games

☐ 10-color pen — eliminates need for 10
single pieces

☐ Soft houses and occupants

ADVANCE ARRANGEMENT

☐ Order kiddy meal — ask in detail what will be
served — consider alternative adult meals.

☐ Seating — at the window your child can see out,
but at the aisle can get out and in without
disturbing other travellers. Drinking liquids is
good for them, so there will be bathroom trips.
Most children look out the window a limited
amount of time. If you are on an international
flight, avoid sitting near the smoking section — try
to book a non-smoking flight. Sit halfway to the
lavatories. Close is convenient but the traffic will
inhibit their sleeping.

PART 5.²

HINTS

☐ Don't plan activities of your own. If you make
your child your "activity," you, your child and the
other passengers will have a good trip. Be
courteous toward your child. A parent who is
too tough on a normally reacting child does not
create sympathy for either of them. Go with the
behavior of your child as best you can. You can't
send him to his room.

☐ The crew is busy with a predetermined schedule
and it does not include child sitting.

☐ Adults with children may always board first. It is
the best way to get settled. Waiting and deplaning

last is also a good idea. The crew then has time to fetch the stroller from wherever they stowed it.

Do not pack: crayons that break and smear; toys that make external noises; toys with sharp edges; scissors; games with loose parts to fall on the floor; no nuts or hard candies — if the plane lurches, child can swallow and choke.

Smaller children may be allowed to sleep on the floor space in front of your seats. After checking with crew, first put down a blanket then as he/she stretches out, put your shoeless feet on the seat.

PART
5.²

CONTINUED

Airplanes and Children Alone

See *Airplanes and Children* — page 138

PART
5.³

HINTS

For security reasons, don't put a child's name in big letters, or their address — home or destination — on outside of backpack. Put name address and telephone number on the inside. In a case of emergency, a rational adult will look inside. Put address of home and destination and who to contact at each place.

A backpack for carry-on works well because it leaves the hands free. Make certain it closes well across the top with a zipper or velcro. Just a flap allows items to tumble out.

Summer: leave room inside backpack for outerwear garment.

Winter: attach gloves to the coat. It is nearly impossible for the child to remember them. Upon arrival, a child will be concerned with getting off the plane and not being left behind. Children don't look under seats for forgotten items. Parents do.

For the first trip alone, arrange with the airlines to board your child yourself and help him/her settle in.

Put copies of the important names and numbers your child needs to have in the checked luggage.

Baby Goes Visiting

PART
5.⁴

Taking a baby visiting to a house where there are no babies? Bring with you what you need to make the visit easier.

EQUIPMENT

- [ ] Baby chair/car seat
- [ ] Baby food in containers
- [ ] Bib
- [ ] Bottle with water
- [ ] Bottle with formula
- [ ] Change of clothes
- [ ] Cup — plastic for drinking
- [ ] Diapers — disposable
- [ ] Formula plus 1 extra serving
- [ ] Pacifier
- [ ] Playpen — many portables double as baby bed. Use it at home occasionally to make it familiar to baby
- [ ] Plastic bag to take home or throw away a dirty diaper
- [ ] Teething ring
- [ ] Toys — 10 small toys and cloth books
- [ ] Wipes — disposable or wash cloth in zip-lock bag

WASH
Maybe

EQUIPMENT FOR OVERNIGHT VISIT

- ☐ Baby bed — portable
- ☐ Blanket
- ☐ Mattress
- ☐ Sheet
- ☐ Bunting to wrap up sleeping baby or use blanket
- ☐ Night light
- ☐ Pajamas

PART
5.⁴

Camps: Day

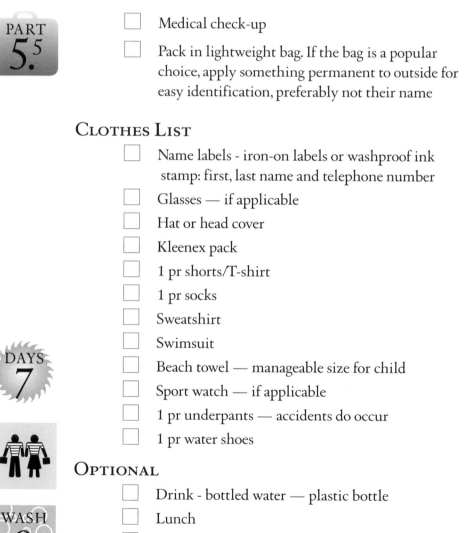

PART 5.⁵

- [ ] Medical check-up
- [ ] Pack in lightweight bag. If the bag is a popular choice, apply something permanent to outside for easy identification, preferably not their name

CLOTHES LIST

- [ ] Name labels - iron-on labels or washproof ink stamp: first, last name and telephone number
- [ ] Glasses — if applicable
- [ ] Hat or head cover
- [ ] Kleenex pack
- [ ] 1 pr shorts/T-shirt
- [ ] 1 pr socks
- [ ] Sweatshirt
- [ ] Swimsuit
- [ ] Beach towel — manageable size for child
- [ ] Sport watch — if applicable
- [ ] 1 pr underpants — accidents do occur
- [ ] 1 pr water shoes

DAYS 7

OPTIONAL

- [ ] Drink - bottled water — plastic bottle
- [ ] Lunch
- [ ] Treats to share - children need icebreakers, too

WASH 0

☐ Disposable camera to take pictures themselves —
write name and address on the camera

Sports Equipment — Ask in advance

☐ Baseball glove

☐ Fishing gear

☐ Tennis racket

Hints

■ At the end of each day allow child to review the list
and repack what needs to be replaced.

■ On one of the last days of camp include a pencil
and a small address book to record addresses and
telephone numbers.

■ Leave the chewing gum and the jewelry at home.

PART
5.⁵

Camps: Overnight Camp

PART
5.⁶

CLOTHES LIST

- [ ] 7 pr underwear
- [ ] 7 bras (if wearing)
- [ ] 7 pr socks/footies
- [ ] 2 pr pjs/sleepwear
- [ ] 7 T-shirts
- [ ] 7 shorts
- [ ] 2 pr jeans
- [ ] 2 sweatshirts — one with hood
- *OR* [ ] 1 sweater and 1 sweatshirt
- [ ] 1 pr canvas shoes
- [ ] 1 pr hiking shoes
- [ ] 1 pr of thongs — rubber
- [ ] 2 swimsuits
- [ ] 1 rainwear — poncho or light waterproof jacket
- [ ] 1 baseball cap or visor for shade

DAYS
7

BACKPACK OR SMALL BAG -
FOR TRAVELLING TO CAMP

- [ ] Bar of soap with plastic case
- [ ] Camera and film
- [ ] Comb/brush
- [ ] Glasses/sunglasses
- [ ] Insect repellent

WASH
0

☐ Identification

☐ Kleenex

☐ Medications/prescriptions — homeopathic: arnica 6x for bruises and falls

☐ Personal items

☐ Sunscreen — number corresponds to your child's skin

☐ Colored zinc for nose

☐ Toothbrush

☐ Toothpaste

EQUIPMENT

☐ Sleeping bag

☐ Pillow

☐ 2 pillow cases

☐ Beach towel

☐ Bath towel

☐ Washcloth

☐ Laundry bag

☐ Flashlight with batteries

☐ Pad and pencils

☐ Home-addressed stamped postcard

OPTIONAL

☐ Musical instrument - consider value and usage

☐ Sports equipment: baseball, soccer, tennis, hockey, lacrosse, fishing gear, equestrian: hat, boots, saddle

☐ Inexpensive, waterproof sport watch

HINTS

▪ To decide which kind of luggage to pack it all in, think about storage space at camp. Use soft luggage - duffle bag if the camp gives cupboard space and

PART

5.⁶

CONTINUED

nothing is to be stored in a suitcase under the bed/bunk. Use hard-sided luggage if cupboard space is not available and luggage will serve as primary storage.

☐ Use iron-on labels or washproof ink-stamp and imprint the child's first and last name and telephone number.

☐ Do not allow your child to take expensive watch or valuable jewelry.

☐ Consider leaving the Walkman and cd's at home, too.

Car Travel with Children

TOILETRY KIT

- [ ] Add to Toiletry Kit - *see How To Pack Toiletry Kit — page 187-189*
- [ ] Motion-sickness pills

HINTS

Backpack or duffle bag per child. Use this to pack all the personal items they may need while in the car.

Car seat - for any child unable to sit in an adult seat. Car seats are all not equal, check carefully before renting or buying. Line the seat with shearling; warm in cold weather, cool in hot weather.

Remember to stop at supermarkets. Pack a picnic in the summer and use the city and state parks. In the winter you can park in a school or church parking lot. Please don't litter, throw it away or take it with you.

Plan ahead for games involving the passing scenery outside. There are good books with suggestions.

Rotate positions for everyone. In some countries no one under the age of 12 is allowed in the front seat. Ask when arranging for a car abroad.

Tapes of interest to children are classical music

tapes to which stories can be made up as you all listen. It is a great way to introduce young children to this music and challenges the imagination of the parents. After some practice, let the children tell their own stories of what they hear in the music. Surprise.

☐ Window shades to block the sun in hot weather.

☐ Don't allow any body parts to be stuck out of the window. Don't store anything on the back shelf.

PART

5.⁷

CONTINUED

Ski Vacations with Children

TOILETRY KIT

- ☐ Sunscreen — a must for little faces
- ☐ Zinc is good for small noses

CLOTHES LIST

- ☐ Après-ski boots
- ☐ Face mask which can serve as neck warmer
- ☐ Fanny pack
- ☐ 2 pr mittens
- ☐ 2 hats
- _Or_ ☐ 1 helmet
- ☐ 1 ski parka
- ☐ 1 ski pants — padded
- ☐ 6 turtlenecks
- ☐ 4 pr ski socks
- ☐ 2 pr thermal underwear
- ☐ 6 underpants

EQUIPMENT

- ☐ Ski Boots
- ☐ Boot bag
- ☐ Poles
- ☐ Skis
- ☐ Ski bag

APRÈS SKI CLOTHES

- ☐ Belt
- ☐ Casual outerwear jacket
- ☐ Gloves
- ☐ Hat
- ☐ Shoes
- ☐ 4 shirts or tops
- ☐ 4 pr of pants/jeans
- ☐ 4 sweaters
- ☐ 1 swimsuit — many resorts have a pool
- ☐ 1 sleepwear/T-shirt
- ☐ 4 socks
- ☐ 4 underwear
- ☐ Scarf for jacket

OPTIONAL

- ☐ Special holder for ski ticket
- ☐ Ski lock

HINTS

- ▩ Buy your children full-length ski suits only as a last resort. Remember they have to go the bathroom, and it all has to come off.

- ▩ Buy their boots at the slope if possible, especially if you are going far away from home to ski. Check boot size each season for each child.

- ▩ Until they are old enough to sweat, they can wear the same shirt twice without washing.

PART

5.⁸

CONTINUED

☐ If your children are young and you have more than one, buy their clothes in the same color schemes. Each year when passed on, or as part of the outfits are replaced, they can be mixed and matched without looking like hand-me-downs.

☐ Remember at some point they will have to go to the bathroom, by themselves. Make the suit easy to get off and on.

☐ Look for plastic zippers on jackets. They are not as likely to hurt little faces when they stick their heads in their jackets for warmth while skiing.

☐ Sew in label with resort address and parents' name.

☐ Helmets are a must.

PART 6

What to Pack

for Additional Family Members:
Pets

Pet Travel: General

EQUIPMENT

- [ ] Bottle of water
- [ ] First-aid book for pets
- [ ] Pooper-scooper/plastic bag. Required in all cities
- [ ] Familiar food and treat

HINTS

- If travel plans include your pet, investigate if it will be welcome in all the places you will visit or stay.

- Check your specific air carrier for rules and regulations or call the Air Transport Association of America for information: 202 626 4000.

- Airlines require cages that meet certain standards. Pets travel as baggage or cargo. Book direct flights. This limits exposure to weather conditions at interim airports and additional take-offs and landings.

- If shots, immunizations or inoculations are required carry with you the current documentation. Rabies shots must be given 30 days in advance of border crossings.

- As a rule, in the U.S. pets are not allowed in amusement parks, bars, department stores, grocery stores, hotel rooms, malls, public parks, restaurants, theme parks, zoos.

☐ Use a cage for car travel too. A roaming animal is a hazard. Never leave a pet in a closed car in summer, or unheated car in winter.

☐ On ocean liners, pets are caged in a special section and there is a veterinarian on duty.

☐ For foreign travel with pets call the U.S. Customs office at JFK airport in New York: 718 995 2113.

☐ Countries in Europe vary about pet acceptance. Some city centers don't allow dogs. In hotels where they are allowed, an additional charge is added to your bill.

PART
6.1

Pet Travel II: Accompanied by Owners

PART
6.²

■ This list assumes pet is welcome at your destination

EQUIPMENT

- [ ] Bottle of water
- [ ] Bowl for food
- [ ] Bowl for water
- [ ] Collar/leash
- [ ] Canned food (just this time)
- [ ] Dry food
- [ ] ID tag for pet with current address, phone number
- [ ] Pet carrier for transportation
- [ ] Placemat/paper towels
- [ ] Pooper scooper/plastic bag
- [ ] Portable scratching post — cats
- [ ] Sweater (if applicable)
- [ ] Toys/treats

HINT

■ Groom pet prior to visit. Less hair will be left after you are gone. Sprays are available to cut down on dander and lessen allergic reactions.

YOUR NOTES AND COMMENTS

PART 7

What to Pack

for Rental Vacations

Renting a Summer Beach House

PART 7.1

These lists have no amounts. This is assumed to be a car trip and each person decides how much they need. Fill in the numbers that suit you.

TOILETRY KIT

- [ ] Add to Toiletry Kit - *see How To Pack Toiletry Kit — page 187-189*
- [ ] Sunscreen — highest number
- [ ] After-sun cream

CLOTHES LIST

- [ ] Bath robe
- [ ] Beach jacket
- [ ] Beach hat
- [ ] Scarves
- [ ] Shoes
- [ ] Shorts
- [ ] Socks
- [ ] Sleepwear
- [ ] Sunglasses
- [ ] Sweatshirt/sweater
- [ ] Swimsuit
- [ ] Thongs
- [ ] Tops
- [ ] Underwear

DAYS 7

WASH *Anytime*

EQUIPMENT LIST

☐ Alarm clock for next to bed

☐ Boxed games for evening instead of TV

☐ First-aid kit

LINENS LIST

☐ Sleeping bag for each child

☐ 1 pr sheets for each adult bed

☐ 1 pr pillow cases for each person

Or ☐ 6 dishtowels

☐ 2 bath towels for each person

☐ 1 washcloth for each person

☐ 1 beach towel per person

Or ☐ 2 beach towels and 1 bath

If table linens are not provided, paper is an option

☐ Napkins

☐ Placemats

☐ Tablecloth

☐ 1 roll of toilet paper per person per week

☐ 1 roll of paper towels per 3 days

☐ Note pad/pen/pencils to make lists

PART
7.1

HINT

▨ Kitchen should be equipped with plates, cups, flatware, glasses, pots, pans and basic cooking utensils.

TO THE BEACH

☐ Beach bag

☐ Beach chairs

☐ Beach mats

☐ Beach towels — one per person

☐ Inflatable boat with oars
☐ Lifejackets

CONTENTS OF BEACH BAG

☐ Books and magazines
☐ Bottled water
☐ Cookies
☐ Fruit
☐ Paper cups
☐ Sandwiches
☐ Sunglasses
☐ Sunscreen
☐ Zinc

PART
7.1

CONTINUED

HINTS

☐ Take along a cookbook. It makes meal planning and grocery shopping easier.

☐ Take your most-used kitchen utensils. If you need them, taking them is cheaper than buying new ones.

☐ Pack a cooler to take food to the beach. Fill it there with bagged ice to keep drinks cool. At the end of the vacation you can take the leftovers home. You can also put wet clothes in it.

☐ Blankets and pillows are usually part of the house equipment.

Renting a Mountain Home in Winter

A mountain home is better outfitted than a mountain cabin because a mountain home caters to the skiing crowd. Kitchens will be more complete, linens and maid service are often included.

PART 7.²

If it is a "cabin," supplies are sparser and warmer clothes and additional blankets are needed.

TOILETRY KIT

☐ Toiletry Kit — *see How to Pack Toiletry Kit — page 187-189*

CLOTHES LIST

☐ Backpack
☐ Belts
☐ Boots, not shoes
☐ Heavy gloves
☐ Hat that fits snugly
☐ 3 pr jeans
☐ Jacket — coats are more cumbersome
☐ Robe
☐ Scarf — wool
☐ 3 long-sleeved shirts
☐ 6 pr socks
☐ 3 sweaters

DAYS 7

WASH *Anytime*

☐ Sleepwear — flannel

☐ Slippers — floors are cold and boots are left just inside the door

☐ 6 turtlenecks to wear under shirts — 4 if washing is an option

☐ Underwear — long top and bottom

HINTS

PART
7.2
CONTINUED

▨ Avoid leather clothes — they are not warm. Plan to wear clothes in layers.

▨ Will there be a fireplace there, and is wood available? What is the main source of heat? It helps to know when selecting clothes to pack.

▨ If linens are not included, blankets and pillows usually are. It is important to know quantity of blankets.

EQUIPMENT LIST

☐ Sleeping bags for children

☐ 1 pr sheets per bed

☐ 1 pr pillow cases per bed

☐ 6 dishtowels

☐ Bathtowels — 1 per person

☐ Washcloths — 1 per person

SPORTS

☐ *See Skiing list — page 90*

☐ *See Hiking list— page 84*

Renting a Summer Vacation Home in Europe

TOILETRY KIT

☐ Toiletry Kit — *see How to Pack Toiletry Kit — page 187-189*

CLOTHES LIST

☐ *Clothes List — see Part 1 What to Pack: Metropolitan Cities of the World—page 26-28*

INCLUDE IN LUGGAGE

☐ Cookbook of regional recipes

☐ Measuring cups and spoons

☐ Collapsible padded thermo bag for picnics

☐ Corkscrew

☐ Flashlight

☐ Insect repellent/Calendula creme to put on bites

☐ Light socket bug repellent

☐ Net shopping bag for grocery shopping

☐ Tote bag for city shopping

☐ Small notebook and pen for shopping list

OPTIONAL

☐ Magnifying glass (hand-held) for viewing art and buying jewels

DO NOT PACK

☐ Maps — buy them locally

Valuable jewelry — unlikely that there will be a safe

HINTS

PART

7.3

CONTINUED

Linens may not be included in rental price, but can be had for an extra charge per week. Arrange this via the rental agency before your arrival. Ask if laundry facilities are available.

Ask if maid services are included.

Request a list of persons to contact if something needs attention.

Pack sweaters for the evenings if you are in the mountains. Summer evenings are cool. If an alpine wind blows in, temperatures can drop to 40 degrees within an hour and your house probably won't have central heating. If it does, it will be expensive.

Your own country club may have reciprocity with a local golf course or tennis club. If so, arrange for a letter of introduction.

Telephone - if not included CANNOT be installed. Arrange for a USA DIRECT service for use at public phones.

Air conditioning will probably consist of portable fans.

Renting a Home in Great Britain

*See Renting a Summer Vacation Home in Europe —
page 167*

TOILETRY KIT

Toiletry Kit — *see How to Pack Toiletry Kit —
page 187-189*

CLOTHES LIST

Clothes List - *see Part1 What to Pack: Metropolitan
Cities of the World — page 26-28*

INCLUDE IN LUGGAGE

"Y"-shaped hose attachment because many
bathtubs don't have mixer taps. This combines the
hot and cold water to flow together

Adapter plug unique to Britain for hair dryer
and shaver

Raincoat and rain boots

Rain hat/umbrella

More sweaters

Renting a Home in France

PART
7.⁵

■ *See Renting a Summer Vacation Home in Europe* page 167

TOILETRY KIT

☐ Toiletry Kit — *see How to Pack Toiletry Kit —* *page 187-189*

CLOTHES LIST

☐ Clothes List - *see Part1 What to Pack: Metropolitan Cities of the World —page 26-28*

INCLUDE IN LUGGAGE

☐ *Wine Atlas* by Hugh Johnson and a smaller wine book or card chart to take to restaurants. You're right, locals wouldn't be caught dead with such a thing, but unless you know it all, this is a great time to learn. It describes vintages and chateaux.

DAYS
7

☐ *Dictionary English to French - French to English.*

SPORTS

☐ Tennis racket. There are good public courts in France. Take balls and shoes — both are expensive

WASH
1x7

Renting a Home in Italy

☐ *See Renting a Summer Vacation Home in Europe —*
  page 167

PART
7.6

TOILETRY KIT

☐ Toiletry Kit — *see How to Pack Toiletry Kit —*
  page 187-189

CLOTHES LIST

☐ Clothes List - *see Part1 What to Pack: Metropolitan*
  Cities of the World — page 26-28

INCLUDE IN LUGGAGE

☐ Wine guide and cookbook by Burton Anderson

☐ *Dictionary: English to Italian - Italian to English*

☐ Pasta cookbook listing names of sausages

☐ Purchase a bag of world-wide plug adapters — the
  sockets in the walls are not uniform in Italy and will
  be either too small or too big

DAYS
7

HINTS

☐ Utilities will likely be an extra charge, and the meter
  for the renter may not be accurate.

☐ Always use a reputable international agency. Local
  agencies may favor the landlord. Ask for a detailed
  contract and assume nothing. File your contract
  with the local "Ufficio del Registro." Find out about

WASH
1x7

SUNIA the Italian tenants' union before you need them. Rental laws do not apply to short-term leases.

 Italian landlords have been known to be difficult. The landlord may stay in the rental property during your stay, without your advance knowledge. There is little you can do about it. Legal action is a long, drawn-out process and therefore costly. A foreign renter seldom wins.

PART
7.6
CONTINUED

YOUR NOTES AND COMMENTS

SECTION II

How to Pack

How to Pack: the Answers

■ How to pack is directly related to space, clothing fabric and quantity. You have three options for getting your clothes in the container of your choice. You can roll it, fold it or stuff it. Be ready to do all three.

■ How to decide whether to roll or fold? This is simply a matter of testing the fabrics.

■ Rolling works for fabrics with a large or bulky weave, such as sweaters, sweatshirts, and knits, and for wash-and-wear items.

■ Folding is for fine-weave fabrics, including business suits, cotton and linen shirts and blouses, silks and other "precious" fabrics.

■ Stuff it is for shoes, belts and anything else that retains it's shape no matter what you do to it.

Basic Baggage and Luggage Options

BASIC BAGGAGE

Matched luggage does not travel better. But it may be easier for you to spot at the baggage claim. New luggage is not necessarily better than old.

If your travel plans are one-day-one-place, take fewer clothes, less luggage. Only you know the outfits are repeats.

You can carry two bags of relative equal size easier than carrying one large and one small bag.

LUGGAGE OPTIONS

Carry-on luggage. Official airline measurements for under-the-seat-in-front-of-you are 23 x 13 x 9 inches (58.5 x 33 x 23 cm).

If you want to put it in the overhead compartment 36 x 14 x 10 inches (91.5 x 36.5 x 25 cm) will fit. (This may be the official rule, but it is amazing what passengers try to fit into the compartments. You can watch with amusement, unless your carefully folded coat was put there first.)

A small duffle bag is 26 inches (66 cm) long.

A large duffle bag is 48 inches (122 cm) long. First airlines count the number of bags checked, and then the weight. Bigger is sometimes better — up to 70 pounds (30 kilos).

A garment bag 40 inches (102 cm) long is best for suits and jackets. A garment bag 50 inches (127 cm) long is for coats and dresses.

Two 30-inch (76 cm) valises have enough space for 7 days vacation and are a good balance. Don't try to carry a third bag as well.

Children should use a backpack or a rucksack. It leaves their hands free (and helps them to stand and walk straight).

The largest soft-sided bags you can find are best for packing the bulky clothes for a ski vacation.

Boot bags and ski bags should have as much built-in protection as your budget will allow.

Whether to buy fabric, leather or plastic depends on your personal taste and budget.

Whether to take hard or soft-sided luggage depends on transportation and destination. Once you're there, will you stay in one place or move residence frequently? Who will carry it? If it's you, make it light. If it's portered for you, the charge is per piece.

Hard-sided Luggage

1. Place bagged shoes, hair rollers and curlers along the back/bottom of the suitcase. Note how a suitcase stands when it is closed. The heavy items should end up sitting on the bottom which is the back while you are packing.

2. Next, lay your largest clothing items across the flat space formed by the sides of the suitcase. Arms of coats, dresses and suits will be hanging outside the suitcase.

   Lay pants/slacks with the waistband touching one side of the suitcase, legs draping off the opposite side.

3. Roll-up jeans, sleepwear, swimsuits, T-shirts, underwear — everything but shirts and blouses. Place the rolled clothes on top of the flat clothes. A tighter pack means less shifting.

4. Now lay folded blouses/shirts on top of rolls.

5. Fold the ends of the clothes sticking out of the suitcase back over the rolls and the flat-folded clothes. Fold the sleeves of suits, coats, and jackets from the shoulder diagonally. This makes a "package."

6. Stuff belts, small miscellaneous items into the odd spaces and the four corners of the suitcase.

Hints

When folding shirts and blouses, end with the collar in the middle of the fold. Fold cuffs over collar, the cuffs provide cushioning and prevent crushing.

Check heels of shoes before packing. Replace if worn. Check for rips and tears and that zippers work. You only get one chance to make a first impression.

Soft-sided Luggage

1. Pack all shoes, rollers, books at the bottom of the up-right bag. They provide weight and create a flat surface.

2. Roll everything. A suit rolled in the plastic bag from the cleaners will pack nicely but first remove the hanger. Folding is futile as there is nothing to keep the clothes in place.

3. Put the heaviest clothes in first. The top layer will be lightweight fabrics.

3. Pack to give form to the luggage. Lay the rolled clothes side to side. Alternate the direction of the rolls with each layer.

HINTS

The more interchangeable and coordinated individual clothing items are, the better your wardrobe will serve you.

Two shirts of the same color are a good idea. If you spill on one while travelling, you can change before arriving, and it will match your suit.

A Hanging Garment Bag

 So you've decided to take your hanging bag once again. This tried and true luggage piece has been around for years with little change in design — except for someone adding a couple of wheels. This bag works because it is lightweight, conforms to the dimensions of a carry-on and fits into the overhead compartment. If it's your lucky day, you might hang it in the private closet in first class.

1. Lay bag on a flat surface and zip it open completely.

2. Hang all longer clothes — coats, dresses, skirts. Hang blouses over skirts or pants and under jackets. This creates extra padding and helps prevent wrinkles.

3. Cover every other hanger of clothes with a plastic cleaning bag. The bags are easier to reuse and give better protection than tissue paper.

4. The first article of clothing to hang in the garment bag should be the longest one and plastic covered. As you pack, alternate plastic covered and non-plastic covered clothes. Make the last/top item plastic covered.

5. Finally, from the back, bring the longest piece of plastic up and over the top so that your clothes are completely encapsulated in plastic — from top to

bottom, front to back. Secure the ends of the bags under the luggage straps.

6. Pack shoes in the end/bottom. When the bag is carried, the heavy weight is now at the bottom.

HINT

Think of the compartments in a hanging bag as drawers in a chest. One for underwear, one for socks/pantyhose or items that belong together such as two or three swimsuits.

Other Luggage Options

INDIVIDUAL LUGGAGE PIECES

- [ ] Camera bag with strap
- [ ] Cosmetic bag — liquid proof or plastic
- [ ] Document/passport holder
- [ ] Fanny pack
- [ ] Jewelry pack
- [ ] Shoe bags — can be used as buffing cloth
- [ ] Tie holder case
- [ ] Wallet exclusively for foreign currency

LUGGAGE ACCESSORIES

- [ ] Luggage cart
- [ ] Luggage locks
- [ ] Luggage ID tags
- [ ] Luggage straps

SPORT LUGGAGE

- [ ] Bicycle box — supplied by airlines
- [ ] Golf bag — hard shell for air travel
- [ ] Squash/tennis racket cover
- [ ] Ski bags
- [ ] Ski boot bag

TRAVEL ELECTRONICS

- ☐ Travel clock
- ☐ Travel plug adapters

HINTS

 There are clever gadgets you can buy to convert currency, speak foreign languages and do other things, but think seriously if you will use them before you give them space in your limited luggage allowance.

Take only voltage-convertible appliances. If your shaver is battery operated, take extra batteries.

Try to buy a compact travel plug that fits most of the world's systems and is complete in one unit.

OPTIONAL

- ☐ Hat box
- ☐ Train case
- ☐ Train pass case
- ☐ Steamer trunk
- ☐ Writing portfolio

Cosmetics

Cosmetics are a personal choice, but here is a definitive list. Pick up your toothpaste tube and deodorant and look at the size measured in ounces. This is important information and the following list will help you decide how giant a tube of toothpaste or bottle of mouthwash to pack.

To help you get a feel for size, the little bottles the hotels supply in the bathroom are .75 oz. The contents of a bottle of bath gel are sufficient for two baths, a bottle of shampoo, two shampoos. You get the idea, two servings for one person. Decide if you want to take a slew of little bottles, and discard them as you go, or a larger size to last the entire trip.

HINTS

Dobb kits are usual for packing men's cosmetics, but do consider the new, popular, see-through, hanging cosmetic bags. These bags allow you to see what's packed inside through the clear plastic windows. The divided interior contains that leaky bottle and you're not washing the shampoo off your shaver at the next stop. If your quaint accommodations have old fashioned sinks with no shelf space, these hang on the door or on the wall hooks.

Cosmetics/Toiletry Kit: Men

- [ ] 1 oz of deodorant lasts 2 weeks
- [ ] 6 oz (125 ml) of non-aerosol hair spray lasts 4 weeks
- [ ] 7 oz of gel mousse lasts 4 weeks
- [ ] 6 oz of mouthwash lasts 2 weeks used 2x a day
- [ ] 2 oz (59.1 ml) of shampoo/conditioner lasts 2 weeks
- [ ] 3.5 oz (75 ml) of toothpaste lasts 2 weeks used 2x a day
- [ ] 1.5 oz of cologne/aftershave lasts 4 weeks if used 1x day
- [ ] .75 oz is standard size of complimentary hotel samples and lasts 2 days for 1 person

SUPPLIES

- [ ] Acne creme
- [ ] Aspirin — flat pack
- [ ] Baby powder — cornstarch only — works as a dry shampoo. Sprinkle powder in your hands and then run your hands through your hair. Brush your hair. This removes grease adds body
- [ ] Brush
- [ ] Comb
- [ ] Condom(s)
- [ ] Dental floss

☐ Hair dryer — if applicable

☐ Lip balm

☐ Matches: if sharing a bathroom, freshen the air by lighting a match and letting it burn for 3 seconds

☐ Moisturizer/sunscreen

☐ Nail clipper

☐ Nail file

☐ Razor/extra blades, shaving creme/brush

OR ☐ Shaver

☐ Sewing kit: needle, thread, buttons, safety pins.

☐ Shirt stays for shirt collar

☐ Small scissors

☐ Toothbrush

☐ Tube of washing solution — or use the complimentary shampoo in hotel room

Cosmetics/Toiletry Kit: Women

- ☐ 1 oz of deodorant lasts 2 weeks
- ☐ 6 oz (125 ml) of non-aerosol hairspray lasts 4 weeks
- ☐ 7 oz of gel mousse lasts 4 weeks
- ☐ 6 oz of mouthwash lasts 2 weeks used 2x a day
- ☐ 1.5 oz of cologne lasts 2 weeks if used 2x day
- ☐ 2 oz (59.1 ml) of shampoo/conditioner lasts 2 weeks
- ☐ 3.5 oz (75 ml) of toothpaste lasts 2 weeks used 2x a day
- ☐ .75 oz is standard size of complimentary hotel samples and lasts 2 days for 1 person

SUPPLIES

- ☐ Aspirin — flat pack
- ☐ Brush/comb
- ☐ Baby powder — cornstarch only — works as a dry shampoo. Sprinkle powder in your hands and then run your hands through your hair. Brush your hair. This removes grease and adds body.
- ☐ Birth control/Condom(s)
- ☐ Castor oil
- ☐ Curling iron/electric rollers
- ☐ Dental floss
- ☐ Eye make-up

- ☐ Foundation
- ☐ Hand creme
- ☐ Hair dryer
- ☐ Lip balm/lipstick
- ☐ Mascara
- ☐ Matches: if sharing a bathroom, freshen the air by lighting a match and letting it burn for 3 seconds
- ☐ Mirror
- ☐ Moisturizer/sunscreen
- ☐ Nail file/nail clipper
- ☐ Nail polish
- ☐ Nail polish remover pads
- ☐ Perfume
- ☐ Razor/extra blades — skip the creme — use soap
- *Or* ☐ Shaver electric
- ☐ Sanitary needs — pads/tampons
- ☐ Sewing kit: needle, thread, buttons, safety pins
- ☐ Small scissors
- ☐ Tape measure
- ☐ Toothbrush
- ☐ Toothpaste
- ☐ Tube of washing solution — or use the complimentary shampoo in hotel room

Always Carry on your Person when Travelling

Carry-on your Person

- ☐ Bank cards
- ☐ Checkbook
- ☐ Credit cards
- ☐ Insurance information: medical, travel
- ☐ Medicines/prescriptions
- ☐ Passport
- ☐ Transportation tickets and schedule
- ☐ Travellers checks

Carry-on Bag

- ☐ Camera and equipment
- ☐ Cosmetics
- ☐ Jewelry
- ☐ Keys: house, luggage, car
- ☐ Magazine and/or book — for "down time"
- ☐ Walkman/cd player

Optional

- ☐ Earplugs
- ☐ Sleeping mask
- ☐ Travel pillow/neck cushion — inflatable
- ☐ 1 change of clothes including underwear
- ☐ Washcloth — disposable or in plastic bag

Pre-travel Preparations

☐ Make two copies each of the documents listed below.

☐ Take one with you and put it in some other place than in your carry-on luggage.

☐ Leave the other copy at your home with family, at the office or with friends.

☐ Passport(s) — the page with photograph and the printed information

☐ Transportation tickets

☐ Credit card account numbers and telephone numbers to call to cancel if necessary

☐ Driver's license

☐ Health insurance information. Check coverage for where you are going

☐ Prescriptions for medicines

☐ Travellers insurance information. Check luggage liability insurance

☐ Copies of numbers of travelers checks

☐ Itinerary including hotel names and telephones numbers

☐ Important family/friends/business telephone numbers

Passport and Visas

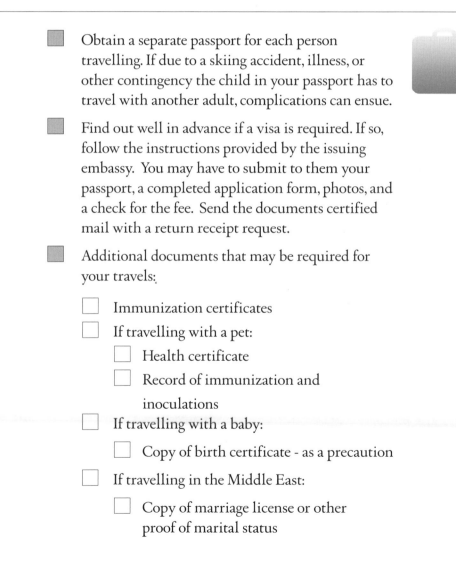

▨ Obtain a separate passport for each person travelling. If due to a skiing accident, illness, or other contingency the child in your passport has to travel with another adult, complications can ensue.

▨ Find out well in advance if a visa is required. If so, follow the instructions provided by the issuing embassy. You may have to submit to them your passport, a completed application form, photos, and a check for the fee. Send the documents certified mail with a return receipt request.

▨ Additional documents that may be required for your travels:

☐ Immunization certificates
☐ If travelling with a pet:
  ☐ Health certificate
  ☐ Record of immunization and inoculations
☐ If travelling with a baby:
  ☐ Copy of birth certificate - as a precaution
☐ If travelling in the Middle East:
  ☐ Copy of marriage license or other proof of marital status

Getting There

Transportation Options

Airplane Travel Hints

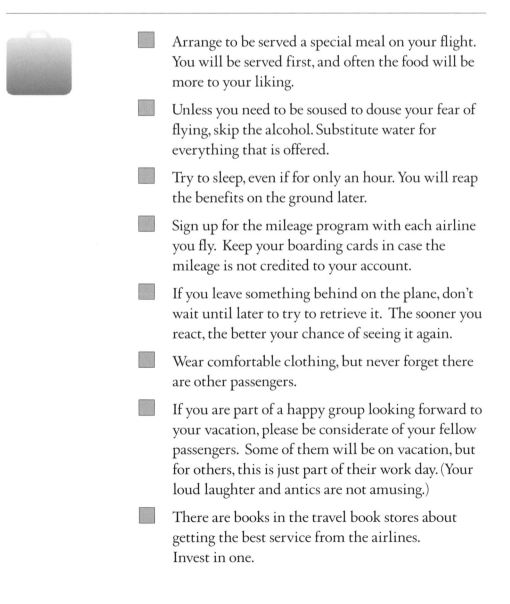

- Arrange to be served a special meal on your flight. You will be served first, and often the food will be more to your liking.

- Unless you need to be soused to douse your fear of flying, skip the alcohol. Substitute water for everything that is offered.

- Try to sleep, even if for only an hour. You will reap the benefits on the ground later.

- Sign up for the mileage program with each airline you fly. Keep your boarding cards in case the mileage is not credited to your account.

- If you leave something behind on the plane, don't wait until later to try to retrieve it. The sooner you react, the better your chance of seeing it again.

- Wear comfortable clothing, but never forget there are other passengers.

- If you are part of a happy group looking forward to your vacation, please be considerate of your fellow passengers. Some of them will be on vacation, but for others, this is just part of their work day. (Your loud laughter and antics are not amusing.)

- There are books in the travel book stores about getting the best service from the airlines. Invest in one.

Car Travel Hints

DRIVING ABROAD

- At time of renting you will need the following:
  - [ ] Insurance
  - [ ] International Drivers License
  - [ ] Rules-of-the-road of the country you will visit —learn the seatbelt laws and parking signs
  - [ ] Road map for first leg of journey

DRIVING IN YOUR CAR
CHECK AND/OR CHANGE

- [ ] Air conditioner
- [ ] Air filter
- [ ] Alignment of tires
- [ ] Carburetor adjustment
- [ ] Cooling system
- [ ] Distributor cap
- [ ] Fuel filter
- [ ] Heating system
- [ ] Ignition points
- [ ] Smog-control apparatus
- [ ] Spark plugs
- [ ] Timing adjustment
- [ ] Tire tread

YOUR CAR'S INTERIOR

- [ ] Auto lock for steering wheel
- [ ] Carpet cleaner/spot remover
- [ ] Car-sick bags
- [ ] Clip board/pencil for notes
- [ ] Coins for city parking meters
- [ ] Coins for tolls
- [ ] Cooler: drinks/snacks
- [ ] Entertainment: books on tape/cd; music on tape/cd
- [ ] Kleenex
- [ ] Maps
- [ ] Paper towels/washcloth
- [ ] Pillows — small
- [ ] Telephone
- [ ] Toilet paper roll
- [ ] Travel laundry bag — keeps dirty clothes away from clean, and if you stop at a laundromat it's all ready
- [ ] Waste bags/car-sick bags for bottles, wrappers and fruit peels
- [ ] Window cleaner

CAR EMERGENCY KIT

- [ ] Adjustable wrench
- [ ] Battery jumper cables
- [ ] Blanket
- [ ] Fan belt and other belts — if applicable
- [ ] Fire extinguisher
- [ ] Flares
- [ ] Flashlight
- [ ] Fuses

☐ Jack
☐ Key light
☐ Lug wrench
☐ Owners manual
☐ Pliers with wire cutter
☐ Pocket knife
☐ Radiator hoses top and bottom
☐ Rags
☐ Screwdriver with interchangeable types and sizes
☐ Spare tire — new or good

OPTIONAL

☐ Wheel locks

HINTS

■ If driving time is longer than one hour, buy an automobile association membership. These organizations provide all types of on-road services including towing when you need it. They also help with trip planning if you visit their offices. Travelers checks, maps and hotel/motel/restaurant listings are free to members.

■ Clean the car inside and out before packing.

■ Check the major components before setting out. Either you or a garage should do an inspection. The time and money spent in advance is worth the alternative of time lost due to a breakdown, towing and costly repairs — if available. Also think of dealing with travelling companions who are unhappy. If alone, think of what the consequences could be.

■ Cooler box. Eating at restaurants while travelling can be expensive. Every city and town has grocery stores — too bad they aren't marked on the road as restaurants are — shop there for picnic foods. The cooler stores what you don't eat.

 Cellular telephone and battery. Sign up for "roaming" services outside your service area. Travellers to isolated places find this a necessary piece of equipment.

Car Travel in Winter

 See Car Interior — page 200

 See Car Emergency — page 200

ADD

- [ ] Blankets
- [ ] Chains
- [ ] Gloves
- [ ] Lock defroster — carry the spray can with you when you park the car — it won't do any good if it's locked in a car with frozen locks
- [ ] Matches
- [ ] Snow shovel
- [ ] Snow tires
- [ ] Thermos with warm, not hot, liquids
- [ ] Umbrella - if there is an emergency and the second person is standing outside to assist
- [ ] Window scraper
- [ ] Window washer fluid — you use more due to dirty roads

HINT

 Some cars use more fluids in the winter. After service ask your garage if the following are needed: brake fluid; hydraulic fluid; oil. Carry extra.

Taxi Tips

In the U.S. most taxis have meters. If you are unfamiliar with the ride, ask someone in advance at the airport, the train station, or wherever you step in, the approximate cost of the ride you plan to take.

In Washington D.C. the taxis do not have meters, and are regulated by zones. You can ask the dispatcher the approximate price of the fare. At National airport, you may request a cab with a meter.

Always note the name and cab number, just take a minute to jot it down. You have to reach for payment so you might as well reach for a pen and paper. *If* you forget something, or for any other reason, you will have the information that will make a difference.

When handing the driver money for the fare, tell him the amount of money you are paying. In big cities the trick is to say that you gave a smaller bill and they are waiting for more money. If you didn't notice, the bills can be switched.

If you received good service, tip! In urban areas, unfortunately being a cab driver is a high-risk job.

In countries where you are unfamiliar with the customs, do ask for guidance before stepping into a cab. Just because it is a cab, is no guarantee of safety. Every airport has an information desk that can give you additional information. You can also seek out information before you leave home.

In some countries it is usual to bargain the price before you engage the taxi service. Know this in advance. Ignorance can be costly.

Train Travel Tips

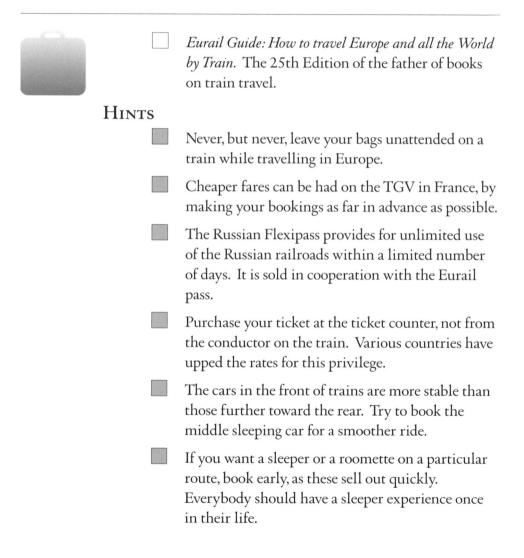

☐   *Eurail Guide: How to travel Europe and all the World by Train.* The 25th Edition of the father of books on train travel.

HINTS

Never, but never, leave your bags unattended on a train while travelling in Europe.

Cheaper fares can be had on the TGV in France, by making your bookings as far in advance as possible.

The Russian Flexipass provides for unlimited use of the Russian railroads within a limited number of days. It is sold in cooperation with the Eurail pass.

Purchase your ticket at the ticket counter, not from the conductor on the train. Various countries have upped the rates for this privilege.

The cars in the front of trains are more stable than those further toward the rear. Try to book the middle sleeping car for a smoother ride.

If you want a sleeper or a roomette on a particular route, book early, as these sell out quickly. Everybody should have a sleeper experience once in their life.

YOUR TRAVEL AND TRANSPORTATION HINTS

Before Leaving

Taking Care of the Home Front

Before Leaving: the House

ARRANGE

- [ ] Mail to be held at the post office for the duration of your time away
- [ ] Indoor plants - put in the bathtub with 1/2 inch of water per two weeks
- [ ] Lights to come on and go off
- [ ] Care of the garden. Tall grass says "no one here"
- [ ] Neighbor to keep an eye open for unusual activity around your house

CANCEL

- [ ] Daily delivery of newspaper

CLEAN UP

- [ ] Bathroom, bedrooms and living areas
- [ ] Put away the clothes you decided not to pack
- [ ] Kitchen: dispose of perishables and wash dirty dishes
- [ ] Put away extra knickknacks usually left out — they only collect dust while you are gone

UNPLUG

- [ ] Small appliances and electronics
- [ ] Iron and put a note by the luggage that you did

HINTS

 The neater you leave your house behind, the better. If something unfortunate does happen while you are absent, it is easier to identify missing items. Lack of clutter makes for speedier solutions.

 Lock the garage doors

Information about your House

The following list is either for your house-sitters, good neighbors, or whomever you have entrusted to keep an eye on things.

Fill in the company name, phone number and contact person

☐ *If the heating goes out:*
Company ....
Phone number ....
Contact person ....

☐ *If the pipes freeze:*
Company ....
Phone number ....
Contact person ....

☐ *If a repair is needed:*
Company ....
Phone number ....
Contact person ....

☐ For the garden:
Company ....
Phone number ....
Contact person ....

☐ *For the swimming pool:*

Company ....

Phone number ....

Contact person ....

☐ *For the security alarm:*

Company ....

Phone number ....

Contact person ....

☐ *Local police department:*

Phone number ....

☐ *Local fire department:*

Phone number ....

Hints for the House Sitter

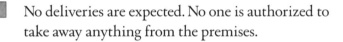

- ■ No deliveries are expected. No one is authorized to take away anything from the premises.

- ■ If the phone rings while checking on things, don't say "they're on vacation," reply, "they are not here at the moment" and ask for a name and number.

- ■ If your house sitter is manually turning on and off the front door lights, remind them not to forget and leave them burning during the daylight hours. That is a dead giveaway.

YOUR HINTS

Addresses

Addresses for Information

CAR

American Automobile Association
Tel. 800 336 4357

CRUISES

Cruise Lines International Association
500 Fifth Avenue
New York, NY 10110
Tel. 212 921 0066

CUSTOMS, FOR INFORMATION ON WHAT YOU CAN BRING BACK

U.S. Customs Service
Public Information Office
Washington D.C. 20044
Tel. 202 566 8195

DISABILITY, TRAVELLERS WITH

Society for the Advancement
of Travel for the Handicapped
347 Fifth Avenue
Suite 610
New York, NY 10016
Tel. 212 447 7284

HOTELS, DETAILS ON ACCOMMODATIONS

Hotel and Travel Index Official Hotel Guide

44 Cook Street	500 Plaza Drive
Denver, CO 80206	Secaucus, NJ 07096
Tel. 800 334 2811	Tel. 201 902 1800

INSURANCE
HealthCare Abroad
Tel. 800 237 6615

MEDICAL ASSISTANCE
International Association for
Medical Assistance to Travellers
417 Center Street
Lewiston, NY 14092
Tel. 716 754 4883

PASSPORT RENEWAL
(first-time applicants must apply in person)
National Passport Center
P.O. Box 371 971
Pittsburgh, PA 15250-7971
enclose a check for $72, current passport
two identical photos — 2 inches square
completed passport application

SENIOR CITIZEN TRAVELLER
The American Association of Retired Persons
Travel Services
601 E Street N.W.
Washington D.C. 20049
Tel. 202 434 3660

SPAS: WHERE THEY ARE
Spa Finders
91 Fifth Avenue
New York, NY 10013
Tel. 212 431 1616

STUDENT IDENTIFICATION
Council on International Educational Exchange
Identification Department
205 E 42nd Street
New York, NY 10017
Tel. 212 661 1450

TRAIN TRAVEL
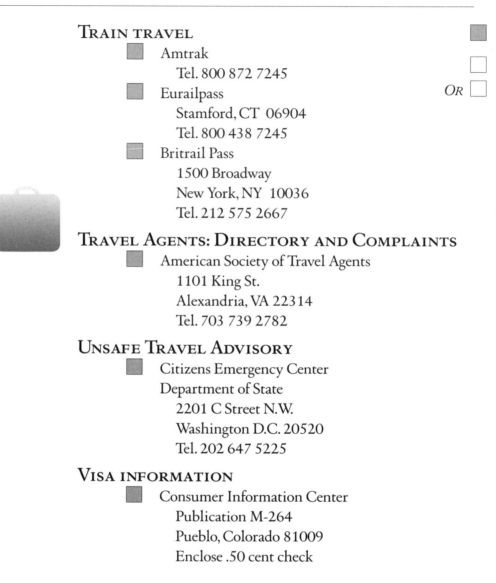
■ Amtrak
   Tel. 800 872 7245
■ Eurailpass   OR
   Stamford, CT 06904
   Tel. 800 438 7245
■ Britrail Pass
   1500 Broadway
   New York, NY 10036
   Tel. 212 575 2667

TRAVEL AGENTS: DIRECTORY AND COMPLAINTS
■ American Society of Travel Agents
   1101 King St.
   Alexandria, VA 22314
   Tel. 703 739 2782

UNSAFE TRAVEL ADVISORY
■ Citizens Emergency Center
   Department of State
   2201 C Street N.W.
   Washington D.C. 20520
   Tel. 202 647 5225

VISA INFORMATION
■ Consumer Information Center
   Publication M-264
   Pueblo, Colorado 81009
   Enclose .50 cent check

YOUR ADDRESSES

Publications
and Books

Publications on Traveling

☐ Travel guides: visit any book store
☐ Michelin guides:
   green: sights to see
   red: places to eat and sleep
☐ *Culturegrams* updated newsletters
   on customs around the world.
   Culturegrams
   P.O. Box 10777, Golden, CO. 80401-0610;
   TEL.(800) 528 6279
☐ *Quick Point* 400 drawings on a small card
   illustrating needs you may have, to use when you
   don't know the words in another language.
   Pictures are internationally self explanatory.

Books

BOOKS ABOUT THE PLACE YOU ARE GOING

- [ ] *Discoveries* Compact paperbacks by Abrams - Stories especially written for the traveller.
- [ ] Books in the Culinary Journey series by Gwenda L. Hyman
  - [ ] *Cuisines of Southeast Asia: A Culinary Journey through Thailand, Myanmar, Laos, Vietnam, Malaysia, Singapore, Indonesia, the Philippines.*
  - [ ] *The New Cooking of Britain and Ireland: A Culinary Journey in Search of Regional Foods and Innovative Chefs.*
- [ ] *The Mind of the Traveler: From Gilgamesh to Global Tourism,* by Eric J. Leed

AFRICA

- [ ] *Out of Africa,* by Isak Dinesen.
- [ ] *Flame Trees of Thika,* by Elspeth Huxley.
- [ ] *Portraits in the Wild: Animal Behaviour in East Africa,* by Cynthia Moss.
- [ ] *Mammals of Southern Africa,* by Burger Cillie.

AUSTRALIA

- [ ] *Kangaroo Comments & Wallaby Words,* by Helen Jonsen.
- [ ] *The Road from Coorain,* by Jill Ker Conway.

CENTRAL EUROPE

☐ *My First Loves*, by Ivan Klima.

CHINA

☐ *Cathy: A Journey in Search of Old China*, by Fergus M. Bordewich.

CRUISE

☐ *The Golden Age of Travel 1850-1939*, by Alex Gregory.

ENGLAND

☐ Theatre in London
Autobiography of Laurence Olivier

☐ *The Once and Future King*, by T.H. White.

☐ Anything by Evelyn Waugh, Noel Coward, Kingsley Amis.

☐ For Children
The Little Grey Men, by "B.B."
Mistress Masham's Repose, by T.H. White.

EUROPE

☐ *A History of Private Life Volume II revelations of the Medieval World*, Georges Duby ed. Arthur Goldhammer, Translator.

FRANCE

☐ *Long Ago in France:The Years in Dijon*, by M.F.K. Fisher.

HAITI

☐ *Best Nightmare on Earth*, by Herbert Gold.

HAWAII

☐ *Hawaii: The Islands of Life*, by Gavan Daws.

HOLLAND

☐ *An Embarrassment of Riches*, by Simon Schama.

INDIA

☐ *Clear Light of Day*, by Anita Desai.

IRELAND

☐ *The Tenants of Time*, by Thomas Flanagan.

ITALY

☐ *Summers' Lease*, John Mortimer.

JAPAN

☐ *The Lady and the Monk, Four Seasons in Kyoto*, by Pico Iyer.

MEXICO

☐ *Distant Neighbors*, by Alan Riding.

MIDDLE EAST

☐ *Palace Walk*, by Naguib Mahfouz.

POLYNESIA

☐ *Tales of the South Pacific*, by James Michener.
☐ *Typee*, by Herman Melville.
Omoo, by Herman Melville.

RUSSIA

☐ *Nicholas and Alexandra*, by Massii.
☐ *The Death of Ivan Ilyitch*, by Tolstoy.
☐ *Goodnight*, by Andrei Sinyavsky.
☐ *Lenin's Tomb*, by David Remnick.

SCOTLAND

☐ *Kidnapped*, by Robert Louis Stevenson.

SOUTH AMERICA

- [ ] *The Old Patagonian Express: By Train Through the Americas,* by Paul Theroux
- [ ] *Eight Feet in the Andes,* by Dervla Murphy

YOUR BOOKS

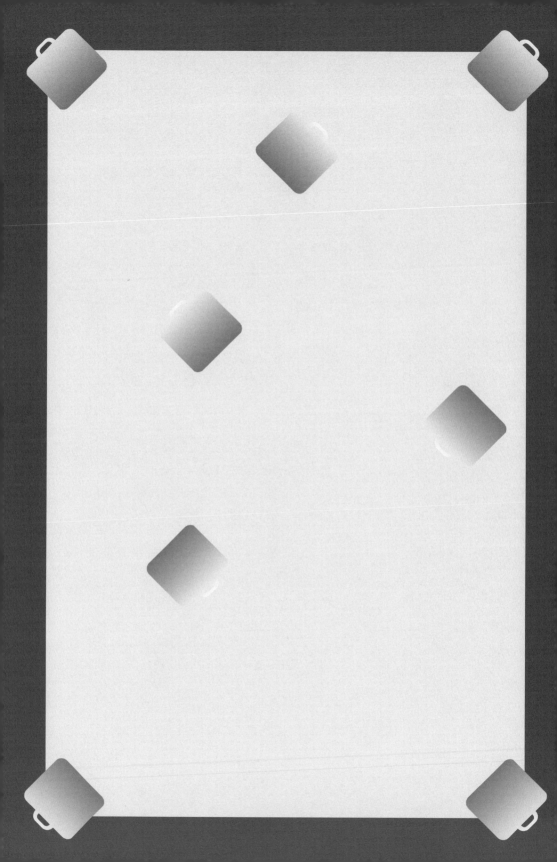

Index

Index

C

J

K

L

M

N

T

If you have a packing suggestion you would like to have considered for the next edition please send it to:

Packing by the Book

Bookit Publishing Ink
PO Box 382
Madison, Va 22727